SAILING

AROUND THE WORLD

THE WRONG WAY

Volume VII

The Red Sea

By
Harold Knoll, Jr.
with
Harold Byler, Jr.

c 2009 by Harold Knoll, Jr. and Harold Byler, Jr. All rights reserved.

No part of this book may be reproduced, stored in a retrieval system,
or
transmitted by any means, electronic, mechanical, photocopying,
recording, or
otherwise, without written permission from the authors.

ISBN: 978-1-4389-1595-1   (paperback)

First published by AuthorHouse 5/21/09

This book is printed on acid free paper.

TABLE OF CONTENTS

Volume I

    Preface

    Introduction

    Chapter I - 1995-6 Lake Michigan to Florida

    Chapter II - 1997 The Bahamas

    Chapter III - 1998 The Caribbean

Volume II

    Preface

    Introduction

    Chapter IV - 1999 Trinidad to the Netherlands

    Chapter V - 2000 Scandinavia

Volume III

    Preface

    Introduction

    Chapter VI - 2001 The British Isles

    Chapter VII - 2002 France and the Mediterranean

Volume IV

    Preface

    Introduction

    Chapter VIII – 2003 The Aegean Sea

Volume V

Preface

Introduction

Chapter IX - 2004 The Black Sea

Volume VI

Preface

Introduction

Chapter X - 2005 The Middle East

Volume VII

Preface -- ix

Introduction --- xi

Chapter XI - 2007 The Red Sea --------------------------- 1

    Michigan, USA, to the Gulf of Aqaba --------------- 1

    Gulf of Aqaba to Hurghada, Egypt ----------------- 19

    Hurghada, Egypt, to Port Gahlib, Egypt ----------- 31

    Port Gahlib, Egypt, to Oseif, Sudan ---------------- 63

    Oseif, Sudan, to Massawa, Eritrea ------------------ 99

    Massawa, Eritrea, to Asmara, Eritrea -------------- 131

    Asmara, Eritrea, to Michigan, USA ---------------- 188

Chapter XII - 2008 Return to Eritrea --------------------- 217

    Trip to Eritrea --- 217

Difficulties in Continuing ---------------------------- 243
End of Cruise and Trip Home ---------------------- 265

Dedicated to:

Harold and Edith Knoll
and
George and LaVonne Visser

ACKNOWLEDGEMENTS

Thanks to the following whose encouragement and support
have been very much appreciated

My wife Vondalee
My parents, Harold and Edith
My wife's parents, George and LaVonne Visser

My crewmembers and the many wonderful people whom I have met
and invited on board for meals and shared stories

All the wonderful people around the world who gave us rides, cars and
bicycles to use, and above all, friendship and advice

Harold Knoll, Jr.

PREFACE

This book is the story of Captain Harold Knoll's voyage around the world. Captain Knoll is a unique individual; he not only has the dreams that most of us have but also has the fortitude and perseverance to attempt to implement his dreams. As a retired schoolteacher, he has knowledge of geography and history. But uniquely, he has the desire to explore that geography and history in person. Captain Knoll, by virtue of extensive study and experience, is a competent sea captain. He has, so far, spent thirteen years in his quest to sail around the world and has accomplished over one-quarter of his goal. Six previous volumes described the first six parts of his voyage. The seventh part of his voyage is described in this Volume VII.

I first met Harold on the island of Martinique in the Caribbean. I later joined him to sail the North Sea, the Mediterranean Sea, the Aegean Sea, and the Black Sea. He is not only a good captain but is also a very good companion. This is a necessary trait on a small sailboat. We never have had an argument. As a result, he has asked me to assist him in publishing his journals. As a personal friend and a long time sailor, I could not refuse. This story is presented in the manner in which it unfolds in Harold's journals.

This book is intended to be a guide to what aspiring world sailors can expect in strange, foreign ports and to enhance their understanding and enjoyment of these places.

Harold Byler, Jr.

May 7, 2008

Brady, Texas

INTRODUCTION

As a young man, I spent years reading stories and looking at pictures of adventures around the world. The National Geographic and later Cruising World, along with various travel lectures, whetted my appetite for travel and adventure. To see new places with different races and colors of people with strange languages became a dream that I actively planned for, saved for, and plotted to achieve.

In high school and college I took courses in French, mathematics, electronics, etc. which were not required for my chosen BA degree in education. My advisors asked how these courses pertained to my educational goals. They did not understand that my hidden goal was to gain all the knowledge and skills necessary to sail around the world. They would have thought I was crazy!

I had another goal that was not too well thought out. That goal was to sire a dozen children. It would not have taken much thought to reveal the fact that "going away sailing" and "raising children" were totally incompatible. Sailing requires freedom from the responsibilities of home, wife, family, and job. Raising a large family requires a large home, a dedicated wife, and a job with a substantial income.

With two occupations, teaching school and farming, I was able to raise eight of my own plus several foster children. This kept me anchored at home with very little time for adventure. I had intended to start my big adventure around middle age, 45-50. However, I married for a second time to a younger woman with three cute little ones. This was poor planning on my part but an adventure in itself! By the time we had raised all of the children, I found myself at age sixty with a mind ready to travel but a body that was a little less willing to climb mountains, dive for lobster, or hike a rainforest.

Before tying the knot for the second time, I did ask some critical questions. Do you like the water? Yes! Would you like to sail? I think so! Would you go around the world? Sure, why not! I not only asked questions but I tested the waters. She liked to swim, fish, and boat. We went out in the worst storms in the smallest boat that I could find. My future wife was calmer, more collected, and less subject to panic than I was. She showed a tendency to take over as Captain while I knelt in the bilge bailing like mad to stay afloat!

During the first year of our marriage, my wife bought me a small 8-foot sailboat called a "Snark". She had watched me for some time sailing an old homemade vessel that was more submarine than sailboat. I had spent more time in the water than on deck. The slightest mistake resulted in a dunking in polluted Lake Macatawa near Holland, Michigan. I learned to tack, jibe, trim sail and most of the basics of sailing with very little help other than the knowledge that to make a mistake was to be tossed into the cold, muddy water. I learned fast under these conditions. The Snark, a foam and fiberglass wonder, proved to be an improvement. It was faster, better equipped, and more seaworthy. It was much drier but still willing to toss me overboard for the slightest transgression. I learned a lot more about sailing from the Snark.

Next came an old Catalina 22. Compared to the Snark, it was a dreamboat with a small cabin containing all the conveniences of home: a stove, sink, water tank, and porta-potty. Now my wife and girls took a real interest in sailing and we spent many days and nights aboard. Things were crowded but happy!

The next logical decision was to invest heavily in a good sailboat capable of going out for long trips and eventually around the world. I sold property and saved for a down payment. In February of 1988, we spent a weekend at the Chicago Boat Show. We fell in love with and purchased a "Gulf 32" motorsailer made by Capital Yachts in California. We found out later that the company was going bankrupt. We became owners of a big, heavy, fully equipped sailboat with a large 40-hp diesel engine. Photographs of this sailboat have been shown in previous volumes of this series.

In talking with fellow sailors about routes around the world, it soon became evident that my ideas were different from those of most people. My plan started with the normal route of going south down the rivers to the Gulf. From this point on, I chose to depart from the norm and take the "wrong way around" according to the wise men of the marina set. The reasoning for the conventional route is based on the prevailing east winds. It is, of course, more difficult and slower to sail against the wind. However, I had no intention of risking my boat and my life crossing the Atlantic against the prevailing winds. My plan included a freighter ride across the Atlantic to Europe for my boat and me since sailing across would entail paying a crew and furnishing food as well as the wear and tear on the boat for a considerable period of time with nothing to see but ocean.

From Florida, I planned to visit the Bahamas, Hispaniola, Haiti, The Dominican Republic, Puerto Rico, the West Indies to Trinidad, and then to cross the Atlantic to Europe. I planned to explore the British Isles, Scandinavia, the European Continent, and then travel the Mediterranean Sea, the Aegean Sea, the Black Sea, and the Red Sea. I wanted to visit Spain, France, Italy, Greece, Turkey, and the Eastern Mediterranean countries, then go down through the Suez Canal and continue eastward.

Retirement couldn't come soon enough! At 60 years of age, the incentive of a lump-sum buyout pushed me over the rough spots and the decision was made. Goodbye home – bring on the world! In September of 1995, we traveled down Lake Michigan from our new home in Montague, MI, to explore the world! Volumes I, II, III, IV, V and VI cover the succession of trips from Lake Michigan, U.S.A., to the Red Sea. The route covered by this Volume VII is shown in Figure 1 on the next page.

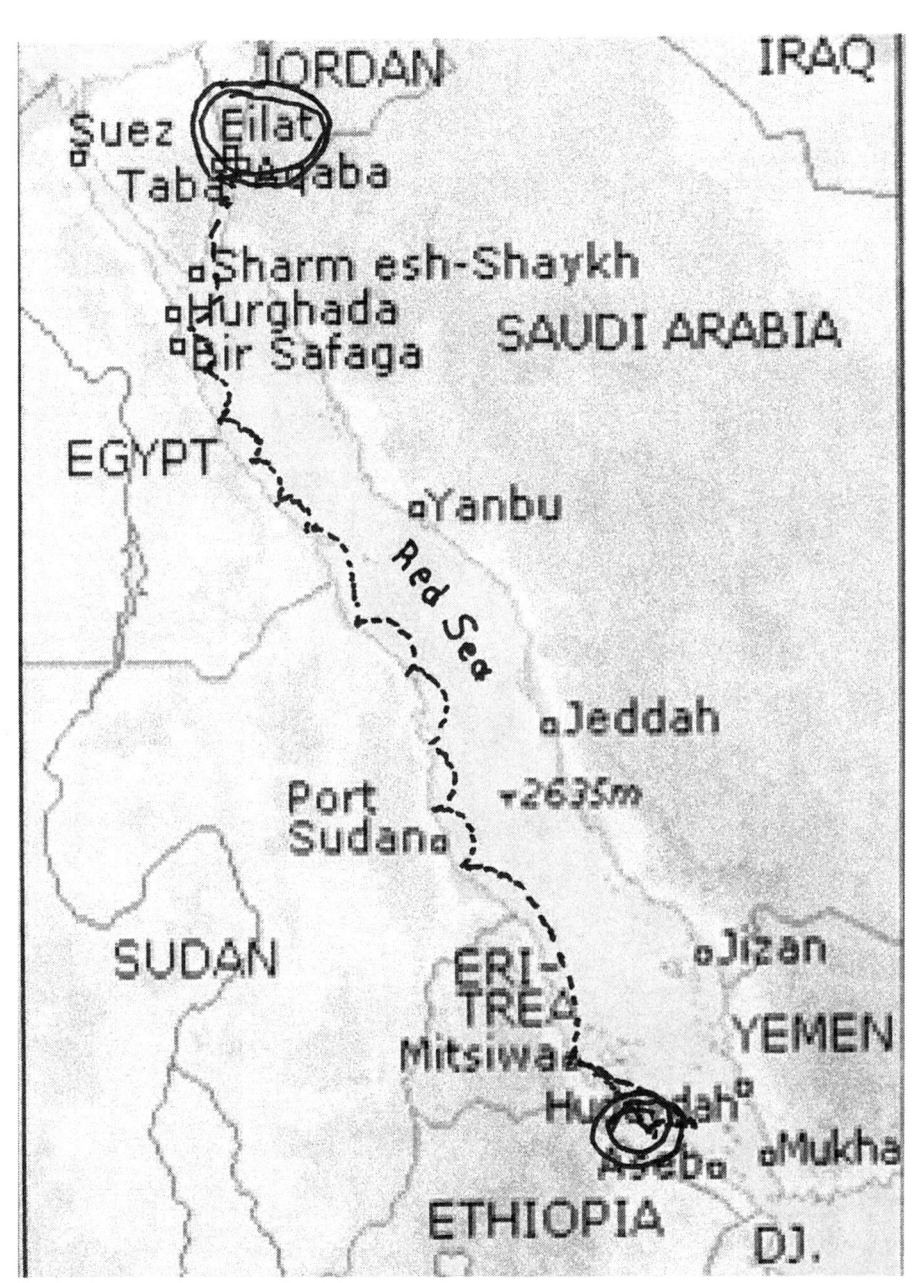

Figure 1

Red Sea Route

My Sailboat, the "Idyllic"

"Idyllic" is a hard name for Americans to pronounce and use. The French call it "Edillic". The English use it often in conversation and do not have any problem whatsoever with it.

"Idyllic" is a Gulf 32 motorsailer with 32 feet overall length and a 10-foot beam. She has a low cabin roof and good sailing characteristics. This is a heavy displacement boat with a full keel. It displaces 7.5 tons with about 3.5 tons in the keel. It sails a little slow with light winds but is very upright and keeps a good course. The rig is a sloop with a two-reef mainsail, working jib, 150% genoa with Harken roller furling, and a small storm sail. At first I planned on converting it to a cutter rig but found this unnecessary, especially in strong winds where I very seldom even use the mainsail.

A large 40-hp Universal diesel engine weighs the stern down slightly more than desirable but comes into its own on the rivers and canals of the US and Europe. It starts and runs great, is very economical, and is reliable.

The cabin below contains a double-vee berth in the bow, a berth partially under the starboard cockpit, a settee berth and a table which folds up to create a double berth in the main saloon. There is a full galley with a CNG cook stove that was later converted to butane (called camping gaz in Europe). There is a hot (manifold) and cold water system in the galley and in the head, which contains a lavatory, shower, and toilet. There is also a freshwater shower in the cockpit. The freshwater tank holds 75 gallons, and the diesel fuel tank holds 75 gallons, which on some occasions is too much fuel storage. However, this is a valued asset when running the motor full time on canals and rivers. The boat has wheel steering both on deck and below. Her electronics include two GPS's, a big Garmin 75, and a small Magellan Pioneer that I found to be very adequate, extremely accurate, and reliable until it was submerged, taken through the German metal detectors and subjected to the Y2K disruptions. There is a VHF radio permanently mounted below by the chart table. I now have small handheld VHF that can be taken to the cockpit for convenience. Figure 2 shows the "Idyllic" hull and sail plan. Figure 3 shows the deck and cabin plan.

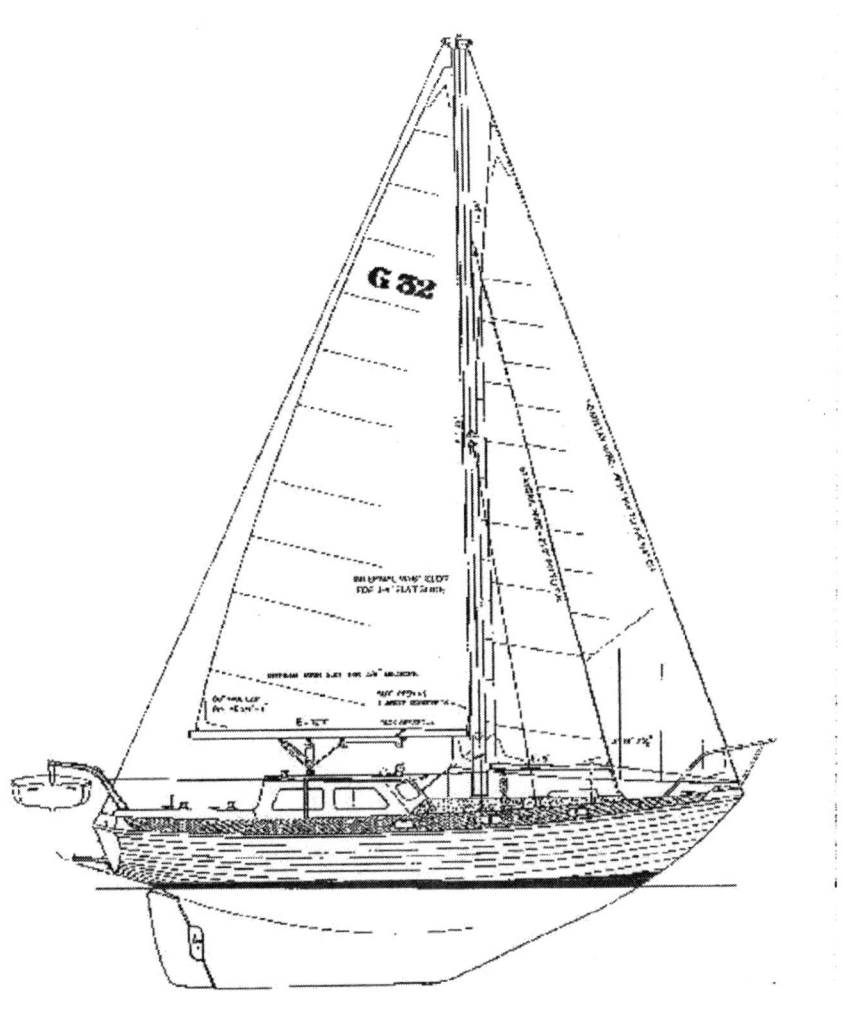

Figure 2

"Idyllic" Sail and Hull Plan

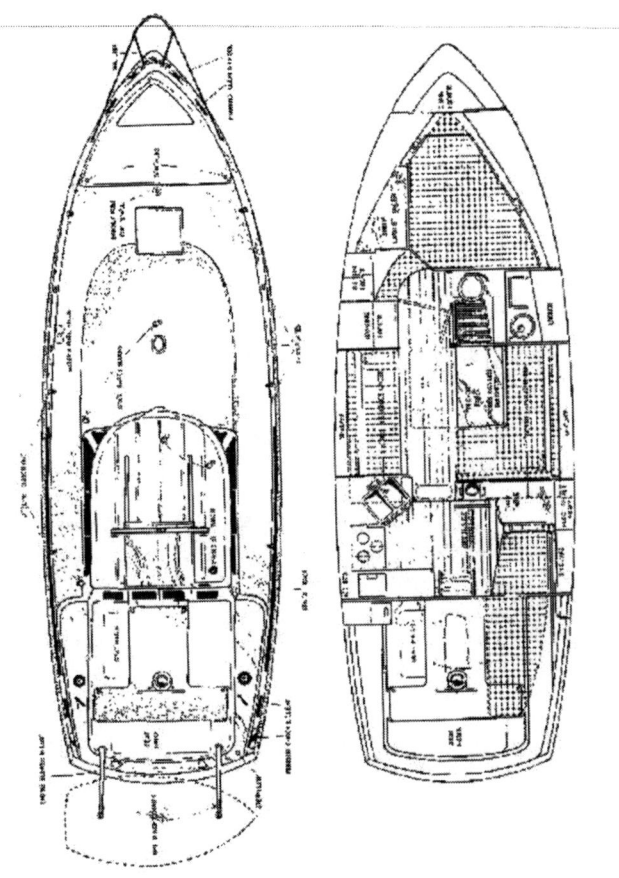

Figure 8

"Idyllic" Deck and Cabin Plan

Figure 3

"Idyllic" Deck and Cabin Plan

CHAPTER XI – THE RED SEA

Michigan, USA to the Gulf of Aqaba

I left my home in Montague, Michigan, to rejoin my sailboat, "Idyllic", that I had left in Eliat, Israel, at the top of the Gulf of Aqaba, and continue my trip around the world. I had previously arranged to join the Vasco da Gama, Red Sea Rally (RSR) group of boats to travel down the Red Sea from Eliat, past Somalia and Yemen, to India. Traveling in the group would provide some security against the pirates who were operating freely in that area. These pirates represent a grave danger to ships, both large and small.

Allen Borsonaet from Montague, who planned to see Israel and dive on the reef at Sharm El Sheikh, traveled with me in a rented car to Chicago on November 1, 2007. From there we took a ten-hour flight to Paris and a three-hour connecting flight to the Ben Gurion Airport in Jerusalem, Israel. This trip was much too long to sit in one place and was very tiresome.

Eli Mor, my former crewmember from Israel, was waiting for us at the airport exit with a big smile and a Shalom. We traveled in Eli's car to his home in Mazkert Batya where his wife, Ilana, was waiting. After much talk, I began to drift off and Ilana had a bedroom waiting for us. The next day, November 2nd, we sailed out of Ashdod, Israel, in Eli's 32-foot sailboat. We had a short but beautiful sail on a

Figure 4

Eli's boat in Ashdod, Israel

flat Mediterranean Sea with a 10 mph wind. The water temperature was 80 degrees and the air temperature was 85 degrees. I was still suffering from jet lag and remember very little about the sail. I bought a new Danforth anchor at the marina and had it shipped to Eliat, Israel.

The next day we ate breakfast at the fancy spice restaurant where Eli's daughter, Yael (biblical name of the woman who killed the leader of Israel's enemy), works on weekends, when she's not serving in the army. Afterwards, we went to Jerusalem to show Allen the sights,

On November 4th, we awoke at 4:30 a.m. to pack for the bus trip to Eliat. Eli drove us to the bus station where we took Bus 303 across the Sinai desert to Eliat, arriving early in the afternoon. We grabbed a quick sandwich at a sidewalk café where, for 28 ILS (New Israeli Shekels) ($8 US), we hired a taxi to the "Idyllic" at the shipyard. The ship appeared to be in good shape after being neglected for two years.

On closer inspection the next day, I found a large amount of sand phosphate and dust covering both the outside and inside of the boat. I had left two hatches open for ventilation; this was a mistake that allowed dirt to penetrate the inside of the cabin. The sand phosphate came from the shipyard where they load large freighters on a regular basis. It was hard to remove the dust as it had accumulated in layers that had become a hard, caked-on mass after two years' time. We washed and scrubbed with great vigor, finally succeeding in the removal of most of it.

We went to town the next day via Bus #15 for 4 ILS ($1.15 US) each and bought a small amount of food to tide us over until we had more time to provision. Later we took a dip in the sea as the air, at 95 degrees Fahrenheit, was very hot. We did some snorkeling that Allen enjoyed very much, since it was his first time to try it. Afterwards, Allen left for town and I fell asleep to avoid the heat. Later we pumped up the inflatable dinghy and planned to install the floor in it the next day.

Tuesday, I cleaned the boat and cooked chicken wings for dinner, with fresh vegetables and orange juice. The next day Allen went to town for groceries and was gone a long time. When he returned, he felt sick to his stomach. I bought some blue anti-fouling paint and began the process of painting the bottom of the boat. I finished half the boat with a lot of help from Allen while he drank a six-pack of beer. I went swimming afterwards and saw many colorful fish while diving.

I had been having trouble with my laptop computer. Fortunately, I met Robyn from "Yofy" and she let me use her computer. She and her husband, Menahem (Manny), had planned to sail to Egypt but their motor wouldn't start, so they had to cancel the trip. After all their preparation, their starter solenoid had burned out and they were unable to find a new one. Later, I met Tommy on his motorboat from Stockholm; he was joining the Rally also. He was willing to help with my computer. When I talked to David, the shipyard manager, he told me they planned to launch "Idyllic" the next Monday, or no later than Tuesday. I was skeptical about that.

Figure 5

Harold with David

On Thursday, November 8th, Allen became increasingly agitated and actively depressed. He started leaving the boat for longer and longer periods of time. Then he started talking about a bus ticket to Sharm el Sheik, Egypt, in order to go home. He finally came right out and said he was leaving, after only four days in Eliat. He had made arrangements to take the bus to Tel Aviv and fly home. I took Allen to town and helped him find the bus station with a place to store his luggage, as he was six hours early in his rush to get home. He said he was homesick. We had a sandwich together and talked pleasantly for a while. Later, Allen walked passed the bus stop where I was waiting to go back to the boat, after shopping for groceries.

That afternoon, Jonathon (Joe) Guemas and Nicolas (Nico) Detournay arrived from Brittany, France, as planned, to be crewmembers. We talked for a long time and they decided to sleep on deck, as it was beastly hot down below in the "Idyllic". Later Eli Mor showed up with his friends who came to the Gulf of Aqaba to dive with the handicapped club. It was really good to see him again. He is a great friend.

That night I went to investigate lights on the waterfront and found David, the shipyard manager, and his family having a Sabot BBQ. I was immediately invited to join them. David, his girl friend and her son home from the army, David's son, and a cousin were there. The meal consisted of: first the salads and hor d'oeurves, then cheap BBQ meat such as chicken hearts, livers and wings, and then special sabot meat patties, followed by fish and steaks. Halfway through the meal, the fire died and it was necessary to go back to town to get more

Figure 6
The New Crewmembers
Joe and Nico

charcoal, which took a long time to restart so they could begin cooking again. They asked many questions about my travels and my home, especially about snow and ice, my family, and how my daughter Vonna was doing.

The next day we removed the labels from the cans and boxes so the Arabs would not know we had visited Israel. If they knew, we would not be able to enter their country. The boys unfortunately, against my advice, allowed their passports to be stamped in Israel making them unusable in Arabic countries. They had to find ways of replacing them at the French Embassy in Tel Aviv.

Manny and Robyn stopped by with a spray nozzle for cleaning my fuel tank. They also brought along charts for me to copy, covering Eliat to India, from a man named Rene, who I had not yet visited. This was a wonderful gift from these great friends.

I had several small successes the next day. I went to town with the boys looking for the Amergas Company, which we soon found with no trouble. I was unable to get butane for my cook stove and purchased a tank of propane, which worked fine. I had thought my stove required butane, but this was not true.

After returning home and taking a short nap, I saw a man hand-pumping diesel fuel into his tanks. I asked if I could borrow his pump and he said, "yes". I then proceeded to immediately pump out the 2-year old fuel in my tank. Unfortunately, replacing it in Israel was going to cost me over 4 ILS ($1.15 USD) a liter. On the way back, David stopped me to say that "Idyllic" would be put on the rail to be

Figure 7

Joe Painting the Bottom

launched at 9:00 a.m. the next morning. Tuesday had turned out to be a very productive day for me.

We got busy and started to clean and polish the boat with wax, from top to bottom and front to back; a big job, which the three of us accomplished in one day. Next we washed some more of the dust away. At noon, Joe made pasta that was very good. Although I was very tired, I took the boys diving for the first time in their lives. The swimming was excellent. We saw many beautiful tropical fish all around us. By the end of the day, we were worn out and my muscles were so sore I could hardly climb into bed. Both boys were from Brittany by the sea but they said there were not many fish there and the water was colder. We spent the evening talking over plans and recuperating. The nights in Eliat were warm at 70 degrees with the days at 90 degrees plus.

Time was passing quickly and we were still on land. However, much was being accomplished. The boys, Joe and Nico, seemed to be working well, although they had not been tested at sea. They were smart, very willing to work hard, and were very willing to learn. They were both studying English and spent a great deal of time in the French-English dictionary looking for translations and pronunciations. The shipyard was moving very slowly, which I expected, with boats constantly coming and going, getting in the way of any movement on our part. A promise of Monday or Tuesday had been given, but I had serious doubts about that. Time was not an issue now that Allen had departed, as we no longer had to be in Sharm El Sheik on the 18th for his diving. We did, however, need to meet the Red Sea Rally boats on the 24th in Hurghada, Egypt.

I had a promise of moving "Idyllic" to the railroad car at 9:00 a.m. Tuesday. Several hours after that time, we finally got started. A Mid-East problem of major proportions developed when we tried to hook up the trailer, on which Idyllic had sat for two years, to the tractor. The tractor was much too modern, being the largest Volvo truck produced, and much too long to attach to the trailer. After a very long Hebrew discussion among the five men of the shipyard, the Arabs, and the tractor driver, a very primitive method was devised, which entailed resting the trailer on boards placed on a large round tool on the tractor. Thus, without actually hooking up, we were able to, very carefully traverse the shipyard to the railway. This was several hundred agonizing yards. Then the boat was next to the railway car that was sitting on the tracks leading into the sea and was ready to be lifted by crane the next morning onto the railway car. We used the rest of the day cleaning the boat, filling the water tank, and test starting the engine.

On Wednesday, I had high hopes of getting the boat into the water. It was near the railway car, which was free to take us unless something unforeseen happened. I arose at 6:00 a.m. to prepare "Idyllic" for launch as promised at 9:00 a.m. They loaded the boat onto the railway car and ran it down to the water, but decided to delay launching it for a day, as the water was rough and there was a strong north wind.

Figure 8
Truck Pulling Trailer

Figure 9

Idyllic on the Crane

Figure 10

Idyllic on the Railway Car

Our stay in Eliat was good, but leaving would be even better. The previous ten days had been hectic and troublesome with worry about finding charts of Egypt, as well as the crewmember's invalid passports containing the Israel customs stamp. That night I visited my very helpful friends, Manny and Robyn, in their boat at the marina and said my farewells.

The next day the launching went well with no problems other than a loose screw allowing fuel to escape from the tank. Fuel is terribly expensive in Israel. I started the engine and we motored north to the port at Eliat to tie up to a buoy just off the beach in order to save the money that we would have to pay to the marina. We found seven buoys but only three were suitable for large boats. The crew had great difficulty catching the ring on the buoy, but after three passes they finally hooked it. After a "petit dejounez", we launched the dinghy and dug out the dinghy motor, oars, and gas tank. Low and behold, after two years, the motor fired on the third pull and worked perfectly during the remainder of my trip.

We took the dinghy to the marina where we tied up to Tommy's motoryacht from Stockholm, Sweden. He invited us on board for coffee. He also helped me program the charts of the world on my computer. He was a great man, very helpful, and the type of person who loves to fix things just for the enjoyment of doing it, refusing all money. Such people are immensely helpful and appreciated.

I woke up to beautiful sunshine in Eliat harbor after a restless night, as every disco in the city played loud music until 5:00 a.m. in

Figure 11

On the Rail Ready for the Sea

Figure 12

Waiting for the Sea

the morning! The first order of business after breakfast was putting on the sails. As the wind was light and there were three of us to help, it went easily and we finished quickly. Both the mainsail and the genoa were installed and we turned into a complete sailboat of the first order.

By 7:00 a.m. we were ready to go ashore and pick up my computer from Tommy. Poor Tommy! He owns an old, 35-foot motorboat that he had sailed all the way from Stockholm, Sweden, to Eliat. It was equipped with every gadget known to mankind. He loved to tinker and was excellent with almost everything electrical and mechanical. He explained his filter system for fuel, which took considerable time and lost me after the third filter. I hope no one has to try to understand this elaborate system without Tommy. He has a computer-guided, navigation system attached to his GPS with a multitude of attachments of which he was very proud. However, just a week before joining the rally when he tried to clean his bottom, he found the propeller, sacrificial zinc, and metal work badly corroded. He believed the neighboring boat had an electrical short that had caused massive electrolysis in the water. He was going to have to remove the propeller and have the boat inspected. He was waiting for the insurance company's compensation. After waiting for two years, he cannot leave until things are settled. I wished him, "good luck".

I talked to Manny and Robyn and then went shopping for canned meat, which is hard to find.

The Gulf of Aqaba to Hurghada, Egypt

We had intended to leave Eliat on Saturday, November 17th; however, Joe had lost his credit card in the ATM so we needed to wait until Sunday to try and retrieve it as Saturday is the Sabbath in Israel. I also needed to buy another battery and wait for Rubin and my gas bottle. These things kept us in port for another day.

>For my purpose holds
>
>To sail beyond the sunset and the baths
>
>Of all the western stars until I die.
>
>It may be the gulf will wash us down.
>
>It may be we shall touch the Happy Isles
>
>And see the great Achilles whom we know.
>
>Ulysses-Alfred Lord Tennyson

Sunday, I called port control for permission to leave. As I already had clearance, there were no problems. I received orders to report to the police dock, which we did. When we arrived, we were immediately met by the police, with customs and immigration officers showing up later. I quickly realized they were going to stamp my passport, so I asked them not to but they insisted. After I insisted, I was given a ride in a police car to their office, where I asked again not to have my passport stamped. I was told that I must. I said no. Fortunately, I finally won the argument.

Figure 13
Leaving Eliat, Israel

Everything was going according to the program except that I was having a hard time coping with all the work and stress of the many problems. Much had needed to be done in a short time. I had felt a lot of pressure and had not slept well worrying about the solutions. Every day the wind had been strong out of the north but today, when we needed it, the wind was flat calm forcing us to use the "Iron Sails" (engine).

We left Israel with smiles and a friendly goodbye. There wasn't enough wind to sail, so we motored south to Taba Heights, Egypt, where we surprised them. They asked if we had called, faxed, or e-mailed in advance and I replied, "No". They said we would have to wait until 9:00 p.m.. I thought this was a punishment, but found out that was when the ferry would arrive and their office would open.

We had arrived in Taba Heights (Mersa El Muqabila) around 5:00 p.m. and it took over five hours to check in to Egypt for a total cost of $169. Taba was a small place but was a very busy port. During the evening, three small ferryboats came in carrying over 300 people. They were all from out of the country and needed security checks. We were processed last!

Taba Custom and Immigration had the usual forms to fill in plus some really interesting questions such as:

      How many stowaways?

      Nationality of stowaways?

      How many passengers banned from Egypt?

      Nationality of banned passengers?

The customs expenses for Taba were:

    Arrival $40 (USD)

    Stay one night $15

    2 month sailing permit for Egypt $60

    3 Visas $54

They requested US dollars instead of Egyptian Pounds. The entire procedure took until after 10:00 p.m. to complete! The boys had not been able to do anything about the Israeli stamp in their passports, but it turned out not to be a problem during any of our travels, in spite of the warnings I had received.

Taba Heights was a new development that had been open for only a short time. It had been built by Orascom, which brought in name hotels, a small marina, and a ferry. The marina had water and electricity available, but fuel had to be carried in jerry cans. Taba was important as it was an entrance port for all of Egypt and was a little less expensive than the others I had visited. There were a golf course and shops for those so inclined.

After 10:00 p.m., it became very quiet and sleep was uninterrupted all night until the morning prayers at 5:30 a.m. It was impossible to miss the prayers, carried at full volume by large loudspeakers right beside the boat. We had planned to sail to Nuweiba El Mazenia that day but the winds were gone and again we had to motor all the way.

The crew was working out fine. They lacked even the most basic experience but more than made up for it with their enthusiasm, strength, willingness, and ability to learn rapidly. Nico, on duty at the helm, almost ran down a fishing boat that he did not see until we had passed it. We were three miles off shore and apparently he was not watching at all for a considerable period of time.

We motored into Nuweiba Harbor and anchored next to the Ro Ro Ferry dock. We had just anchored and started to relax when the Captain of a large Navy boat asked us to up anchor and motor out to him to show our papers. The captain kept saying, "Don't be angry". Next, the police showed up in a launch to check our papers and Egyptian Sailing Permit. They gave us an OK. I asked several times for permission to go ashore and they ignored me. Finally, since I had not received an answer, I said, "I'm going ashore". They firmly said "No".

We anchored again and had a restless night with no wind and with "Idyllic" rolling in the swell, followed later by a wind from the south with high waves, all quite unusual. Fortunately, the harbor was protected from the south by a mountain. The next morning we made use of some extra time by oiling the teak on the inside of the boat. We had almost finished, except for the sole, when the south wind died and we decided to weigh the anchor and leave. We departed Nuweiba at 10:15 a.m. for Dhabab. We were under sail the entire way, 36 miles at six knots before a strong wind out of the North. Coming into Dhabab harbor on Tuesday, I hit a stone reef, although it was well marked, had boats anchored on it, and was mentioned in the guidebook.

We decided to stay at Dhabab an extra day at the invitation of the police commander who told us we were allowed to go ashore whereas on a previous trip they had refused me permission and there

Figure 14

Nuweiba Beach

Figure 15
Joe Swimming at Dhabab

had been several bombings since I left. The night was very quiet when we tied up to a large buoy in the center of the harbor. I slept well without interruption and woke up at 5:30 a.m. to a beautiful sunrise. We had a good omen that morning when a large osprey landed on the mast and stayed for some time.

We wanted to see and explore the place so we took the dingy to shore and were welcomed by a smiling machinegun-toting policeman. We took a walk on the beach in front of the hotels crowded with tourists. There was row-upon-row of fancy hotels: Hilton, Sheraton, etc. Many of them had sailing clubs and there were over two hundred sailboards, kites, and catamarans sailing on the bay itself. In a backwater bay, there were many types of organized water sports and kites of all kinds were pulling water skiers. We were good spectators, stopping for a soda at an open restaurant, relaxing, and enjoying it all.

We sailed the next day from Dhahab to Gordon Reef near Sharm El Sheikh in the Straits of Tiran, covering a distance of 26 miles in less than six hours. A good stiff north wind pushed us along handsomely, surfing down waves 2-3 meters high at a good pace. We arrived at Gordon Reef and I was surprised to find twenty or more dive boats and a hundred people, where I had the reef to myself on my previous visit the year before.

We tied up to the dive boat "Gigilo" because I thought they were old friends from my previous visit. I found out that more than one boat has the same name. We didn't like the noise and confusion, so we motored over to Tiran Island, Saudi Arabia. We found a sandy

Figure 16
Tiran Strait

spot in the reef and anchored for the night. I took a quick dip to inspect the anchor and search out the surrounding area. I checked out the damage to "Idyllic's" bottom where I had hit the reef the previous day and found only scratches and missing paint. The anchor appeared to be sliding on the bottom, so I let out as much additional chain as I considered safe in such a small, enclosed area.

We had a terrible night at Tiran Island. A dive boat had advised us where it would be quiet, anchoring up against the island, behind the reef, in sand so as not to ruin the coral. All was fine until the wind picked up and became strong, making the anchorage bumpy and dangerous, as we had very little room to swing. Letting out more anchor chain was not feasible in the confined space. However, we found out in the morning that the anchor had slipped into a coral patch and stuck tight. The anchor chain protested, the waves slapped the sides of "Idyllic," and the wind howled in the rigging, making sleeping uncomfortable. The wind held well into the morning at just under 40 knots.

My health was improving remarkably as it always does when sailing. The combination of a Mediterranean diet with fish and not a lot of meat, swimming, walking, and the work of sailing all combine to make a healthier environment. My blood sugar was down to normal after less than a month on the boat!

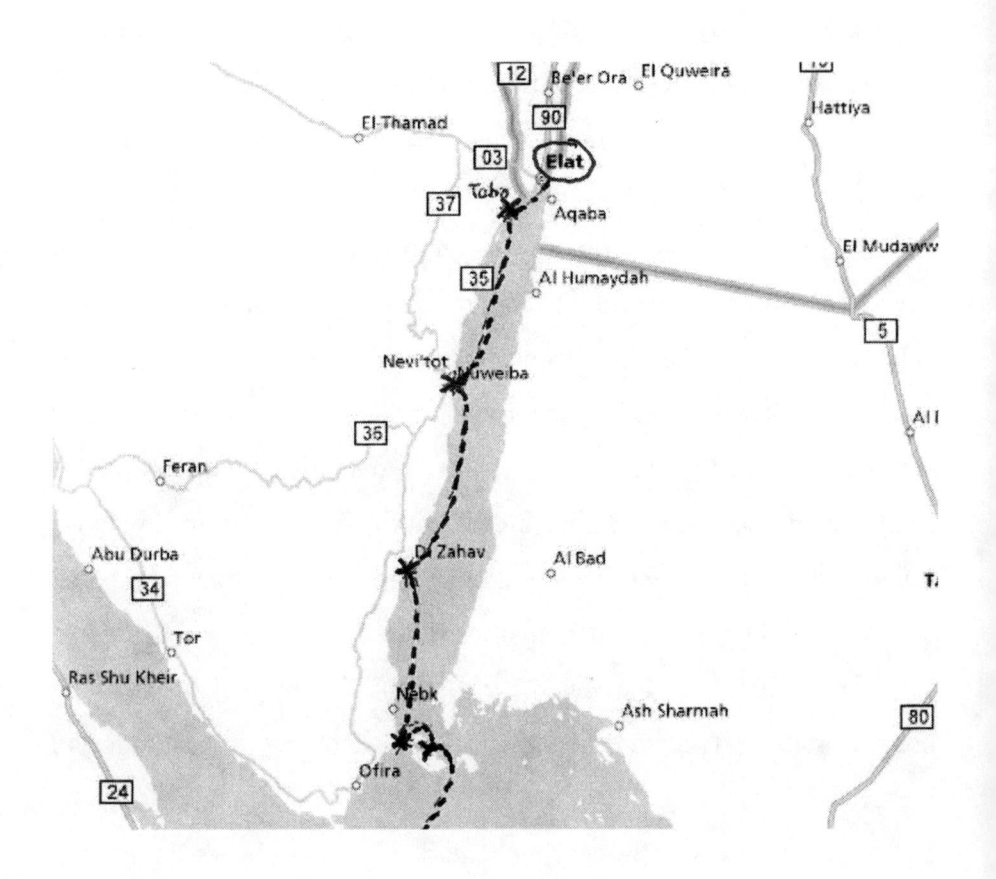

Figure 17

Route from Eliat, Israel, to Tiran Island, Saudi Arabia

Hurghada, Egypt, to Port Ghalib, Egypt

Saturday, November 24th, we left early from our anchorage on the reef at Tiran Island in order to get all the way across the Red Sea to Hurghada, Egypt, during the daylight hours. Immediately after leaving port in the dark, Nico jammed the jib sheet in the winch requiring two of us to extract it. The wind was on our beam at about 20 knots, so we sailed fast toward our destination. The wind died in the late morning, 30 miles out of port, but soon after we started the engine, the wind picked up from the NW and we were able to sail the rest of the way to Hurghada.

Arriving at 5:00 p.m., we asked a fisherman where the marina was, as it was brand new and not in the cruising book or on the charts. He indicated the direction and said, "follow me to the port", which was a real welcome complete with a personal guide boat. However, he did guide us to the old marina. We motored around until we spotted the masts and decorative flags on the Rally sailboats in the new marina where we were met by a marina inflatable that guided us to a berth.

The boys, without experience, were completely baffled as to what was expected at the dock. Joe threw the lines into the water, although the distance to the dock was less than a few feet and Nico was going in circles. The marina personnel were very understanding, as they had seen it all before.

First, I met Lo, the Dutchman in charge of the Red Sea Rally and others in the Rally. Then I tried to sort out the electrical connection, since every port always has a different sized connection. Finally I took a shower, ate, and went to bed, tired after 14 hours at sea.

Lo had negotiated a free week at the Hurghada Marina for the members of the RSR. The Vasco da Gama, Red Sea Rally, had started in Kekova, Turkey, with the 57 boats listed in Figures 19 and 20, bound for India. They had sailed to Cyprus and then to Port Said, where they took the Suez Canal to the Red Sea. I joined them at Hurghada for the trip to India.

Radio Red Sea Rally was heard each morning at 9:00 a.m. whether at sea or in port. The radio first gave the current conditions and then the forecast for the day and the week. Many of the boats had SSB radio, so good weather reports were possible at times. Following the weather report, a report from the committee was given, and then a report from Lo, the chief organizer. Lo had a lot of information about navigation, ports, and officials. He worked closely with marina personnel on questions, complaints and logistics. He coordinated all the activities of the rally at sea and on shore. This was a big job, a lot of which was unappreciated and not really evident. He was very capable, with a smile that won over many opponents without bloodshed. On the other hand, he took a firm stand with those who were out-of-hand or asked too much.

The marina was brand new with most of the buildings still not finished. There were no baths and only a few coffee shops. I took a short walk into the town and it was a shambles with dirt, trash, and garbage everywhere. The buildings were old and falling apart, but the

Figure 18

Hurghada Restaurant

No	Yacht's Name	Nationality	LOA	Beam	Draft	Number of Crew
01	Mistral	Holland	13.40	4.30	0.90	2
14	Rotirik	Holland	10.42	3.42	1.60	Chris en Tineke van Vuuren
21	Vagabond	Sweden	13.00	3.65	1.88	Tommy Westman
25	Miss Cat	France	13.10	4.25	1.90	Jack Croisiere
30	Lady Copellia	UK	16.00	4.60	1.50	Tony Cobb
35	Lunamare	Holland	15.00	3.95	1.95	Frans Groenenboom 1 crew
37	Present	Switserland	12.30	3.90	2.00	Rolf Zahnd Eva Gross-Zahnd
38	Sybaris of London	UK	16.60	4.80	1.50	Per Kjellqvist + 1 crew
39	Alero	Canada	11.40	3.53	1.43	Jean-Louis Levesque Denise Gauthier
40	Lynn Rival	UK	11.49	3.41	1.60	Paul en Rachel Chandler
41	Idyllic	USA	9.99	3.20	1.59	Harold Knoll, Jonathan Guemas, Nicolas Detournay
42	Tamata	Italy	11.00	3.50	0.50	Giorgio Clerici
43	Sepia	Holland	10.20	3.30	1.80	Frank Mooy Marijke van Ekeren

Figure 19

Red Sea Rally Boats, Page 1

44	Reckless of Hamble	UK	12.20	4.10	1.70	T.J.Moore and 1 crew
46	Marvin	Holland	12.00	4.00	2.10	Rien van Zuilen + 1 crew
47	Karl	Ireland	14.50	3.90	1.80	Matthew Hamilton, Phillida Eves + 3 children 12-9-6 years old
48	Mandarina	UK	13.41	3.96	1.98	J.G.E Flint + 1 crew
50	Annka	France	17.60	5.30	2.50	Christian Peguet
51	Dreaming Aruba	Holland	12.70	3.50	1.70	Enzo Nichelatti + 1 crew
52	Alondra of London	Holland	18.00	9.00	1.75	Rene Tiemessen Edith Jellema
53	Gustavus vasa	UK	10.00	3.00	1.70	A.C.Ham and 1 crew
54	Winds & Tides	Holland	10.80	3.85	1.85	Gerben karstens + 2 crew
55	Dionysus	USA	14.00	4.00	2.30	John Jorgl + 1 crew
56	Shaka Zulu	UK	13.4	4.30	1.70	William Smith + 1 crew
57	Panta Rhei	Holland	14.00	4.25	1.75	Willem Steenvoorden

Figure 20

Red Sea Rally Boats, Page 2

Figure 21

RSR Sailers

town was alive with a bus station and seaport crowded with passengers and baggage. I bought a few groceries at a small, dusty market that had only a small inventory. I came back to "Idyllic" for a breakfast of rice, bread, jam, and coffee. I planned to explore more that afternoon.

Arising at 4:30 a.m. the next morning, I washed, dressed, and packed for an excursion trip to Luxor on the Nile River. I joined a tour group for 540 EGP (Egyptian Pounds = $100 USD). This was something I had never done before, but I was required to this time for security reasons. A mini-bus met me and six other RSR sailors, and whisked us off for a short trip down the coast to Safaga, where we rendezvoused with over 100 large buses and 25 mini-buses from all over the west coast of Egypt. The place was jammed with tourists in long lines to the toilet facilities, which were far overtaxed. After a short wait, and surrounded by police security, we formed a convoy over a mile long including the police escort in front and back. Soon, we found ourselves in the western desert traveling at a slow speed, bumper to bumper. We traveled this way through some sand flats, but mostly mountains that were all shades of brown, no green, without a blade of grass anywhere. Arriving at an oasis, we took a 45-minute break.

After more hours of travel, we began to see green and entered the agricultural area of the Nile valley. Lush fields of sugar cane, maize, grass, and vegetables were everywhere. We saw cows, chickens, and goats, as well as donkeys that were pulling carts loaded with people and produce. Most of the farming was done by hand;

Figure 22

Nile River Agriculture

however, the preparing of the soil for planting was accomplished with large modern tractors. Irrigation was standard with water extracted from the large canals by gasoline pumps and then carefully distributed through ditches to every field, as far as the eye could see. Men and women could be seen working in the fields picking and cutting the crops by hand. Donkeys and small two-wheel carts provided the majority of the transportation.

While driving through both the countryside and the city, we saw the police, with shouldered automatic weapons, blocking all roads and entrances to our route. Pedestrians, cars, and trucks all waited behind these armed guards for our convoy to pass, sometimes disrupting their day for a considerable time.

Our convoy arrived with over a thousand tourists, all at once, to the expansive Karnak Temple parking lot. We purchased tickets for 50 EGP ($9.25 USD) and followed the crowd to the entrance. The temple was something to behold with large statues, obelisks, decorations in hieroglyphics, and pictures of the history of Egypt. However, every picture I took contained a hat or the head of the tourist in front of me. One could spend hours marveling at the beauty and historical significance of the 60-acre temple.

Next we traveled to the Valley of the Kings, which I had wrongly understood to be in the Nile Valley. I soon discovered that the site, where the kings were secretly buried, is high up in a mountain valley. The entrance fee was 70 EGP ($13 USD) to see all but the

Figure 23
Karnak Temple

Figure 24

Tower at Karnak Temple

Figure 25

Harold at Karnak Temple

Figure 26

Street of Rams

Figure 27

Colossi of Memnon

Tutankhamun tomb, which cost extra. We rode in a small train up the first steep hill on the way to the tombs, but after that we were on foot. The rock reflected the sun and the path was in a narrow valley between high mountains without any breeze. The sun attacked with vigor from every direction. Walking up such a sharp incline, in sand, was strenuous, but the distance to the first tomb was short.

The tomb entrance had been hidden from human eyes, but was now enclosed with massive concrete walls, bars, and concrete roofs. At the entrance, there were two smiling Egyptians, in local dress, to punch a small hole in your ticket and remind you that photographs were not allowed. Walking down into the tomb corridor, to my relief I was met by cool air. Decorated walls and ceilings were visible the entire way. On the sides, there were small rooms that were also colorfully decorated. Descending farther, there were many chambers before entering the tomb room itself. The mummies were not in evidence, having been removed to museums around the world, especially the Cairo Museum.

As we walked from tomb to tomb, we found them to be spectacular and marveled at the tremendous effort by thousands of men to carve them out of solid mountain, then decorate and paint the chambers, some taking years to finish. A town below the mountain had been especially created for the workers, with many workers' tombs carved into the mountain there. A fertile Nile valley and its green fields were below the workers' town. A short distance away

Figure 28

Entrance to Tombs of the Pharaohs

from the tomb workers' town was the Al-Deir Al-Bahari Temple carved into the side of a mountain. From a distance it resembled a modern hotel.

Only after climbing the tremendous ramp to the temple and seeing the statues mounted in front of the columns, can a person begin to realize the magnificence of the entire temple. The inner room is interesting, but the entire building itself is the really impressive thing. By this time I was worn out from climbing, walking, and admiring all the varied historical sites. One member of our party had already fallen twice and was in pretty bad condition. I was very tired, but far from ready to give up.

For security reasons, our Karnak Temple light show had been canceled and our Egyptian guide made us a proposal. He asked if we would rather see the Luxor Museum or take a sundown cruise on the Nile River. All seven of the tourists in my group voted for the Nile cruise. The Nile River is the largest in the world, over 6600 miles long, supplying Egypt with water and life. Upon entering the Nile Valley, I found greenery everywhere with irrigated crops in profusion on perfectly cultivated fields.

The small ferry boat," Moon Shine", was able to easily hold all of us with plenty of room to spare. Our captain, a young Egyptian in traditional gown and bare feet, started a Yamaha outboard that ran poorly and we went upstream against the current, which I estimated to be about 3 knots. We traveled out into midstream amongst barge and felucca sailboat traffic without any lights, life preservers, or other associated equipment of any kind.

Figure 29

Moonshine Tour Boat

The banks on one side were agricultural, rural, and sparsely populated. On the other side, was a large city with hotels and large buildings with many neon lights and much noisy traffic, in addition to many kinds of ships, ferries, and sailboats on the river. When the sun set, it outlined the palm trees, sailboats, and banks of the river in a golden glow. This was a beautiful sight never to be forgotten. Returning to shore, we walked past the brightly lighted Luxor Temple, but we were out of time to go inside until, hopefully, another trip. We returned to our bus and the convoy home was uneventful, arriving at 10:00 p.m., from an unforgettable day.

After paying only 50 EGP ($9.25 USD) a day for our week's stay, in addition to one free week in a fancy marina, we sailed south on December 1st for Abu Suma. This was a distance of some 30 miles, where we anchored in a fine bay with a beautiful reef and sandy bottom. The water was pure and clean with a shore lined with hotels and tourists. Storm clouds were making a beautiful sunset, but I was sure that no rain would come. Night fell at 5:00 pm and darkness descended very quickly on the perfect setting afterwards.

On the way down the Red Sea, one of the Rally boats, the "Gustavus Vasa" hit a reef and was given up for lost. Sailing the Red Sea has its dangers in addition to the pirates. The reefs are numerous and treacherous, as many have never been charted. When the sailboat, "Gustavus Vasa", crewed by A.C. Ham and his wife, was navigating through the many reefs of the Straits of Gubal, the captain was below working out the coordinates via GPS while his wife was up at the helm. They ran up on a reef with a thud and scraping sound from down under.

They immediately radioed for help and the "Reckless of Hamble", captained by Tim Moore, went immediately to their aid. The situation looked hopeless, as the boat was far up on the reef and out of the water with the tide receding fast. The only thing to do was to try to save as much as possible of the supplies and equipment and then call it a loss. Emptying the tanks and off-loading supplies took considerable time and effort. They left her to her fate, but the next day decided to come back and continue the work for the heaver items.

Upon arriving back at the boat the next day, to their surprise they found her partially afloat. Then began the effort to somehow save her. They raised the sails and Chris climbed the mast to heel her over. With motor running full tilt, the boat was able to bump and scrap, with agonizing groans, across the reef and into deep water, to everyone's relief.

Upon closer inspection, and after diving to inspect her bottom, there appeared to be no holes, but a lot of the fiberglass netting was showing, which would require her to be pulled out of the water for further inspection and major repair. The outcome at that time was unknown, except that their trip south was cancelled. The wife called it quits and flew back to England.

We sailed to Marsa (bay) Abu Makhadio on December 2nd and anchored next to two dive boats and some beach toys. The anchor quickly wrapped around a bommie and I thought it would hold since there was absolutely no wind or waves. During the night however, the wind increased and the anchor dragged across the bottom for a considerable distance, so the next night I added some extra weight behind the anchor. I was not pleased with the new Danforth anchor that I had purchased in Ashdod, Israel.

We had two weeks to go before we were expected in Port Ghalib, so we had plenty of time. At 7:00 p.m. the next night, it became necessary to reset the anchor. I had to rouse the boys out of their bunks and they responded immediately. We added more weight to the anchor and I was sure it would hold, as the 35-knot winds had begun to subside. The sandstorm continued all the next day, giving the anchor another chance to slide. I spent a restful day there with the sandstorm raging on land and painting "Idyllic" a noticeable rust color. The hotels on the north and a reef on the east sheltered us. Finally, we got the anchor to hold by putting out another anchor to help take up some of the strain, in addition to adding more weight ahead of it. To sail uncharted water and follow virgin shores; what a life for man!

We left for Ras Abu Soma on December 6th. When we arrived at Ras Bay, the sand bar looked inviting and we decided to anchor out and not go into the marina. The boys liked the idea, rather than spend money at an expensive marina that would have cost 30 EGP ($5.50 USD) per night. The boys were excellent at saving money and water, which gave me more confidence that we could make the 1100-mile trip across the Indian Ocean, crossing from Oman to India.

On Friday, December 7th, we arrived in the world's greatest den of thieves, Safaga. The city stands on the ruins of the old port of Philotera, built by Ptolemy II in the third century BC. The mountain range inland was both spectacular and beautiful. Safaga was a town known for windsurfing, with plenty of hotels and resorts catering to the crowds. The world windsurfing championships were held there some years back. Diving was also popular, but very crowded in the popular spots.

The next day, I played tourist and did some shopping around town. Safaga was an old town, dirty, full of trash, flies, and more filth than any other town I had seen so far. It was a major port for pilgrims on their life-long-dream journey to Mecca across the Red Sea. There were many large ferryboats based there. With millions of people traveling through, it had become a den of thieves. Demanding "baksheesh" (bribes) from the travelers had become a major game. The main street was lined with shops of every kind and description, even selling girls. All of the shops were small and very busy. Sewage was running down one side street into the main street creating a large pond in which many children were splashing, wading, and playing, as in a swimming pool.

We stayed out overnight, as the main port was not open to foreign boats. We anchored and then tied up to "El Maestro", a dive boat that was not being used at that time and was under some small repair. We intended to stay for a few days, as we were not expected in Marsa Mubarak until the 15th of December.

We went over to visit "Panta Rhei", a South African boat in the Rally with Willem Steenvooren as Captain. We had coffee with him and his passengers, who were all from Rotterdam in the Netherlands. On boarding the dingy to return to "Idyllic", I slid my hand down the rail of his boat and onto the reel of a fishing rod and the hook impaled my hand deeply. There was very little pain but I was hung up with my hand hooked high above my head. The hook was a treble hook, large enough for a whale, or in this case, a homo sapien. Everyone was in shock running in circles, screaming, and shouting when they saw what happened. In spite of the chaos, one fellow grabbed my arm and held on with a vice grip, literally lifting me back on board the boat. He continued his strong grip as I asked for pliers to pull the hook out. One fine fellow showed up with a knife ready to perform surgery. I firmly said, "No". Later, he explained that the knife was only to cut the hook from the line, but I was taking no chances on his intentions. Next, a large electrical pliers were brought out, which I used to first cut the wire leader, and then to extract the hook that was imbedded a surprisingly long way. All through this, there was little pain or blood. I suppose I was in shock, as it all seemed so surreal.

Very little pain developed in my hand; I could write as well as ever. I put antibiotic cream on it immediately and covered it with a band-aid. There was no sign of redness or infection anywhere to be found. I planned to continue to keep it as clean as possible and keep a sharp eye on it for the next few days.

We appeared to have developed a problem, as the fresh water pump was acting as if we were out of water, although we supposedly had over 400 liters in the tank. You never know when the tank or hoses start to leak, as it's hard to detect, especially when bouncing around at sea. The next day, after a bit of investigation, we found the water pump to have a bearing completely worn out. This was a major problem, as a new one would take a lot of time to have shipped in, if it arrived at all. Then I remembered having put a new pump in the bottom of the boat twenty years ago. I dug it out and we installed it quickly. It worked a lot better than the old one.

Nothing else much happened that day, but the next morning I took the dinghy back over to "Panta Rhei" for coffee. They told me a tale about going day sailing and trolling a line for fish one day. A windsurfer came close to the boat and was hooked on the bait at the end of the line. The line ran out until the end, bringing the surfboard to a quick stop and flipping it over in the process. The surfer kept going for a few more meters. They said the Russian probably went back to Moscow telling his friends how he hit this big shark. I spent the rest of the day on the "Idyllic" enjoying the warmth and sun.

I planned to e-mail and shop for fresh vegetables on the 10th, as we planned to leave port early the next morning. The new water pump worked better than the old one ever did. It was a Flo Jet, much quieter with less vibration than the old one which shook the boat when it was running and could be heard all over the marina. I went to both the old town and the new town for shopping, and also stopped at an e-mail café. One restaurant yesterday wanted 60 EGP ($11 USD) for six falafel (an Egyptian food) and today another honest restaurant charged only 3 EGP ($0.55 USD) for the six falafel, a big difference.

We got up very early, awakened by the call to prayer at 4:30 a.m., prepared coffee and untied our mooring line from "El Maestro". We loaded the dingy, gas, and outboard motor in pitch-blackness by flashlight. Just before the sun rose, but had not yet gone above the horizon, we hoisted the anchor and left for Qusier, Egypt. Soon we were sailing with a nice breeze that increased, as time went on, to a really windy day driving us south at a brisk clip. The waves had built up dramatically by the time we reached Qusier harbor! When we tried to anchor in the outer harbor we found the swell to be considerable and decided to try to get in close to the jetty. Soon we were visited by a patrol boat that invited us to moor close in to the jetty. They asked for our papers to be brought to shore first. I took them in the dinghy, but when I arrived there wasn't anyone there, so I returned with the papers to "Idyllic".

We then motored over close to the jetty behind some big dive boats, where we anchored and ran a line to the jetty. About that time, the patrol boat showed up again and dropped an inspector off with us. I gave him our papers and a ride to shore in the dinghy. When we got close, he made a quick leap for the jetty. The dinghy, of course, went smartly in the opposite direction and the customs man fell into the water with his hand grasping the edge of the jetty for dear life! Fortunately, he threw the passports and ship's papers back into the dinghy, saving them from his wet landing. He hit pretty hard and I was concerned that he might have hurt himself, scrambling up out of the water.

The four mosques near the boat made early morning sleep impossible. In addition there was a 100-foot long dive boat preparing to leave port. He needed room to maneuver and it was necessary to move "Idyllic" out of his way. By sunrise everything was quiet and the orange sun was a sight to behold. I grabbed my camera and took

Figure 30

Dock Where Customs Officer Fell In

several pictures of the harbor and the town in the clear air at sunrise. It was a beautiful sight.

When I went to use the bathroom later I found out, that in my hurry in the dark to help the dive boat "Heaven Safir", I had put my pants on backwards. Twelve other RSR boats joined us in the harbor with "Alondra" tying up to the jetty and rafting up with me. Later we went into town and found we were in an old section with much business and a hectic pace in evidence.

There was another beautiful sunrise on the next day, December 13th! Qusier was another ancient port of Leukos Hormos, built to carry the pilgrims to Mecca and extremely important in the old times, up to the 10th century. In medieval times, it was the central shipping point for the Nile valley and the Red Sea. It declined quickly with the opening of the Suez Canal.

Upon going to town the next day, I met up with a group of RSR Italian sailors who said they were going to church and asked if I would like to join them. I immediately said, "yes", with enthusiasm as I had nothing to do and enjoyed new adventures. We soon met a small child who spoke fluent Italian and volunteered to guide us to the church. He turned us all the way around from the direction we had come and led us along the waterfront and through back streets and alleys to an old abandoned industrial area. There were many large abandoned buildings there with equipment inside that could be seen through the broken windows. He explained that this was a very large and important Italian mining company before it was shut down in the

1930's. This explained why many Egyptians in the town spoke Italian, and why so many of the tourists were Italian.

We were led over to a large old building that did not look like a church. The young lad had thought we might be interested in the museum there. Inside, there was a very old collection of fish and animals in glass cases, from floor to ceiling, covered with a layer of dust, in a small entrance room. A curator appeared and was very pleased to see us. I doubt there were any other visitors that year. We walked into the other rooms and were quickly ushered out, as they were offices, with important looking papers and books. Upon leaving, the curator tried to collect money from us, but we were not impressed with his efforts, so he received little or none.

Moving further on through the large building complex, we saw a large building in the distance under construction with scaffolding surrounding it. Upon closer inspection, this turned out to be a new cathedral, swarming with workers inside and out. A beautiful large new cathedral was being erected, a very strange scene in the middle of crumbling old industrial buildings. The boy and a lady inside explained that the Coptic Church had taken over the grounds from the Catholic Church and was building a new church building.

Later in the day the boys took me to a falafel factory and restaurant where we were given a tour of the back room. The owner showed us the machinery and how falafel was made. He carefully explained the recipe of beans, fresh onions, garlic, salt, and pepper, which were all tossed into a large cement bowl. Then, a large machine, run by an electric motor with a belt system, turned a large paddle around and around for a considerable time smashing and mixing everything into a pulp, which was then scooped out by hand into a large bowl and sold to town restaurants. At the restaurants, the pulp was formed by hand (cleaned afterwards by wiping on a dirty cloth) into a small ball and fried until crispy and brown in a deep bowl of olive oil, fired by propane. Then it was scooped out and placed in a pita with vegetables of our choosing and a splash of humus added to taste. This was all for less than $0.30 USD each. Two falafel make a delicious meal for one person.

"Idyllic" was a bit cranky about starting the next morning, as we had burned the lights for a considerable time the previous night. I decided a new, fresh battery was required. I went on RSR Radio and asked for directions to a battery shop. When I found the shop, it was unbelievable. It was a very small, 20x20-foot building with six mechanics working hard on several cars at once. The walls of the building, the grounds, and the men were black with oil. Everyone was working as fast as possible to keep up with the business. A compressed air cleaning of the motor and the motor compartment, with dust flying everywhere, was an additional service included with each oil change. They had every kind of spare part from floor to ceiling on shelves, with larger parts and fluids in a back room, to which I was ushered. Here, I found one wall covered in new batteries. I measured several and picked out the one I needed. After asking the price, I was met with a blank stare; however, after a phone call, they asked for 860 EGP ($160 USD). I told them that in Hurghada, the cost was only 750 EGP ($139 USD). Another phone call was made and 750 EGP was accepted. Then I spotted some outboard gas cans and asked for one of those. In the end, I bought a battery and gas can, all delivered to "Idyllic", at the end of the jetty, by two men in a taxi, for 760 EGP ($141 USD).

Next to this shop was a large souk, selling everything under the sun including live goats and all the products of the Nile valley.

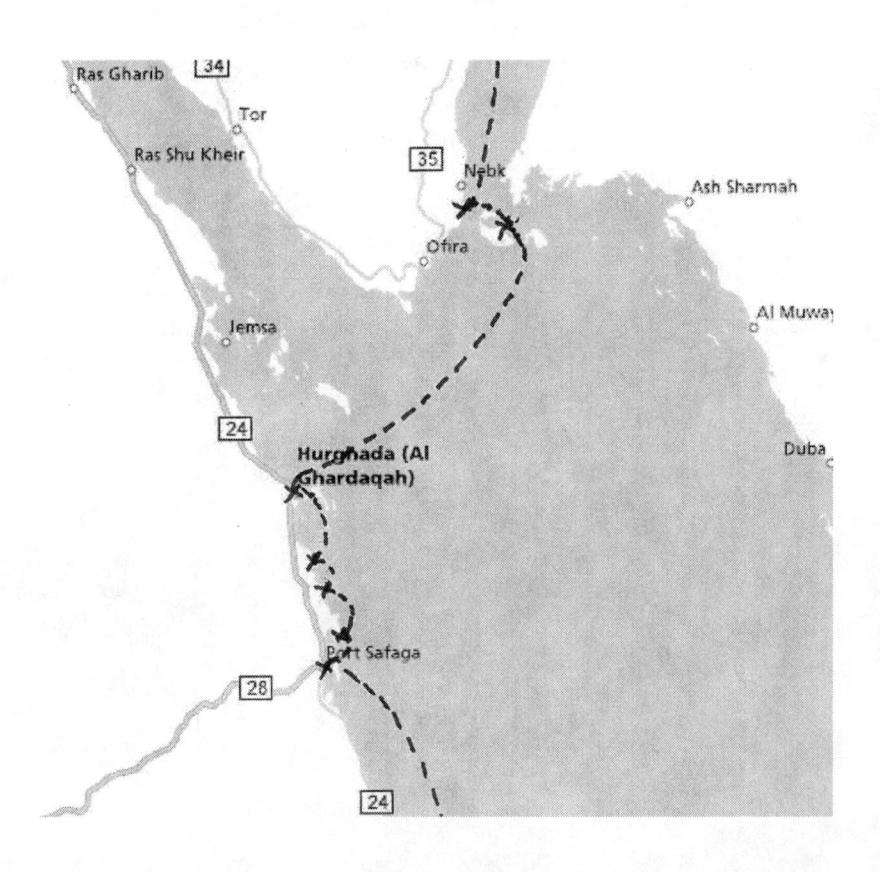

Figure 31

Route from Tiran Island, Saudi Arabia to Port Ghalib, Egypt

Port Ghalib, Egypt, to Oseif, Sudan

On Sunday, December 16th, we had a great downwind sail to Port Ghalib located in Marsa Mubarack. We entered a well-buoyed channel to a brand new city built with money from Kuwait. We radioed port control and answered several questions, to which they already had the answers, having all our information beforehand from the RSR. A marina dinghy came out to meet us, guide us in, and assist in tying us up. We tied up "Idyllic" stern to the wall, Mediterranean style, although most of the other boats were tied up alongside. Those from the rally who had already arrived came to greet us.

Sheerif, the manager of the marina, invited us to a reception that evening and we settled down for a two-week Christmas stay at Port Ghalib. Port Ghalib, a new port of entry, was the first port of entry into Egypt from the south and the last when leaving Egypt from the north. It was a new Kuwaiti development about halfway finished, a beautiful place for the rich and famous, with prices to match. The marina had moorings for 1000 yachts with practically no limit on their size. The marina village was a virtual city with several hotels, an 18-hole golf course, shops, restaurants, pubs, laundry, power station, and a private airport capable of handling the largest jumbo jets, but no shower or bathroom facilities. Two hotel rooms were given to the RSR for showering and washing. Many shops were still being opened and digging was still going on to enlarge the place. Work is

Figure 32
Port Ghalib Map

Figure 33

Port Ghalib and Beach

Figure 34

"Idyllic" Docked Med Style

Figure 35

Marina Docks

continuous on the thousands of acres of desert and 25 miles of beachfront.

I was under the weather, so the reception, including booze and food, was not as happy as normal for me. I left early for "Idyllic" and went to bed. In the morning, a number of boaters sang happy birthday to me, as it was my 73rd celebration. Later in the day, I walked a short distance to the sea and enjoyed the solitude with the beautiful azure water and brown seashore. An Osprey sat on a post and refused to move even though I walked up quite close to him.

On the way back, I was met by Youba and Lloyd, the two Red Sea Rally dogs, who everyone thoroughly enjoyed except for the Egyptians and especially the Egyptian children, as they had never seen dogs like these and were terrified of them. One time Lo, the owner, set them loose on the pier and ten boys ran for all they were worth to get away from them. The dogs thought it was all fun, so they took up the chase and cleared a large dock in no time flat.

On the 18th, we had a captain's meeting, the second of the trip, in which we received a lot of information about the coming voyage between Port Ghalib, Egypt, and Eritrea. Each future port was discussed including navigational problems, port authority's charges, the availability of water, fuel, food, and even the possibility of not being allowed on shore, which is quite common in Egypt. We were warned that the number and size of the sharks would increase as we traveled south, which might sometimes inhibit diving to check the anchor.

Charts were used to show the routes, reefs and navigational markers, which were few and far between. Charts could not be depended on, as they had been made long ago and were very inaccurate. However, the Red Sea Pilot Book made by sailors who sailed these waters, was very professional, accurate, and a godsend to boaters. Charts, electronic computer charts, GPS, navigational aids such as buoys, lighthouses, cairns, and sticks were all to be used but, most of all, reading the color of the water and watching the waves was to be the most accurate technique for navigation. Wrecks of all kinds of boats from small fishing boats, yachts, sailboats, tugs to even freighters, litter the reefs in every direction; some, such as the "Saleem Express", with great loss of life. Many questions were asked and all of them were answered thoroughly and in detail.

The women were especially interested in provisions, none or very little of which was available anywhere. Many times we would have to anchor behind reefs with no one for miles. The deserts offer little for one to eat or drink. The Marsas (bays) are beautiful with clean warm azure blue water and reefs to dive on with many fish that are good eating, but you are not allowed to spear them. Following the meeting, the boys left for El Qusier via bus to buy camping gas as we had determined we would run out before the next fuel stop in Sudan.

I had an incredible night on December 19th. Nadia Kruger, one of the crewmembers from "Alondra", was a singer and had been invited to sing at the local restaurant that night. She invited me to come and listen. Since the boys had gone for the night to buy gas in Qusier, I was alone and bored, so I accepted her offer. The restaurant,

Figure 36
"Mistral" from Holland

Figure 37

"Tomata" from Italy

Figure 38

"Present" from Switzerland

Figure 39

"Alero" from Canada

only a few steps from "Idyllic", was new and extremely modern. Upon entering, I found many divers present waiting for the performance. Soon, Nadia sang and did a professional job with a beautiful voice in addition to playing the guitar very well. The resort manger was so pleased with the performance and the turnout, that he bought us all a drink.

Little did I realize what came next - a belly dancer who immediately caught my attention, as one of my hobbies is the study of the particular detail and aspects of the dance. Soon, she led me by my hand onto the dance floor to join her performance. I did fairly well except my Vasco da Gamma shirt and jeans were not a match for her beautiful costume. Following the dance, another performance was presented with four similarly dressed, male dancers plus one more in a large skirt who began to spin to whirling music that made me dizzy just watching and listening. During his whirling, he performed various routines with his body and a round disc that had a picture of a star on it. A religious sect, "The Whirling Dervish", inspired the act. The night was one to remember as a highlight of Port Ghalib.

The next afternoon, the boys returned from El Quseir with fresh food supplies and two much needed, full bottles of camping gas. They had received information, along with a map, directing them to a man in the town who had filled gas bottles for the ship "Sepia". The return transportation had been a problem for them, as a four-day holiday had begun and no buses of any kind were running, which required them to take a private taxi. But we would have gas for cooking for the next two months with these two bottles.

The next day was stormy with high winds, blowing dust, and sand. On my bike ride through the desert, sand got in my eyes several times and I found that in a gust I could close my eyes for a time and thus prevent eye problems. Of course this put seeing where I was going on hold, presenting some problems such as going over a cliff or hitting a boulder of which there are many scattered about the desert. Riding my bike in the desert was possible with slightly under-inflated tires and a sharp eye to avoid obstacles and patches of fine, quick sand. The route would be circuitous and not fast, but with patience and diligence I could make my way about. In this manner I traveled several kilometers on land and along the seashore. This method of travel was a surprise to me and allowed me to carry more food, water, clothes, etc. On a return trip, the basket would always be full of various treasures found along the way, like a hand crafted fruit crate, seashells, coral, scraps of campfire wood, and much more. Somewhere in the desert a Persian army of forty thousand men was lost without a trace many years ago.

I was invited to the "Present", from Switzerland, to use their computer to e-mail home, which I did with great relief, as I had not been able to get my Internet to work because I left the computer program at home. Later I got together with John and Karen from "Dionysus" of San Francisco and joined in the decoration of our RSR Christmas tree, conceived by Eva on "Present". We took a crooked walking stick of eucalyptus that the boys picked up in Qusier and ran string up and down it to support the decorations. Everyone then made

Figure 40

Christmas Tree

Figure 41

Egypt's Largest Swimming Pool

ornaments out of junk they picked up around the marina to decorate it.

We all got together for a party, set the tree near the hotel, and decorated it with whatever trash we could pick up. It was lots of fun and a crowd of Egyptians gathered. They had never seen anything like it and watched in awe. Christians are crazy, the religion is strange and confusing, and they use trash to worship the birth of Christ!

That night we all got together for a songfest and a Christmas party on "Dionysus", where hors d'oeuvres, eggnog, and spiced wine were served. The boys were missing the fun, as they were off to tour Egypt by foot and by bus. All the food was American with no surprises. Drinks and good companionship were had by all. The owners of "Dionysus", Karen and John, were a bit concerned about everyone sitting on one side of the boat, for fear it would capsize, as over 40 people were aboard. They were a bit paranoid, as the Dionysus had once been sunk at the dock in a hurricane in Florida. It had been raised from the bottom and completely rebuilt.

I attended a Christmas Eve dinner at the marina restaurant where many different kinds of food such as calamari, veal, beef, and chicken were served. I had hoped to either get a menu or to test all of it and report. I will not attempt to list the great amount of food set before us in the buffet dinner. The decorations were vast and unique, consisting of carved gourds, bouquets of pickles, toy houses of pastries, and lights, along with Christmas music.

A large room was full, wall-to-wall, with food of every kind and description. There was one table piled high with breads of all kinds from French bread to American sliced buns, and some I could not identify. Next came one whole wall lined with warming containers of filet of fish, two kinds of beef, rice, and vegetables in ten different containers. Adjacent to this on another side of the room were the deserts, at least 20 platters of various delicious dishes. I concentrated on the wonderful fruits, melon ball on yogurt, star fruit on small round pastry, strawberries, and on and on. Next came the grill with three chefs grilling calamari, steak, kabobs, and two tremendous large roasted turkeys. The calamari was on sticks and I went back for more so often the cooks stopped asking and just piled on more without saying anything. The cost matched the size of the room full of food. The bill was 20 EU ($28 US) plus drinks, 20 EGP ($3.75 USD), including an RSR discount.

    I tried to get out of the ordinary on Christmas day and left on my bike to go north to the other side of the development. The going was rough, as it was all a construction area with sand roads and lots of stones. Upon arrival, I found unbelievable security, but didn't pay much attention, as it was my first time there. Biking through the development, I found very few shops open, maybe two out of a hundred or more. I biked over onto the observation pier and out over the reef where I found a young lifeguard there in the cold and high wind. We talked for a while and I found out he was a college graduate and a lawyer, doing this as a part time job.

    When I returned to land, I saw several large golf carts carrying well-dressed people and I was quickly stopped by security, who explained it was the owner from Kuwait and his managers. They said

Figure 42

Marina Guard

he was the second richest man in the Arab world, spending six to seven billion on this development alone. Since I was hungry, I found a new Pizza Hut open with about ten employees standing around with nothing to do. I shook hands with several before finding a booth. I ordered a seafood pizza for $4 and enjoyed a good American style meal. Soon it was interrupted by the owner of the development and his entourage of 20 people, coming in for a quick tour. He was an elderly gentleman, thin, with balding hair, and a sour looking face, showing much worry and age. Everyone bowed and scraped to him. I tried to get a picture, but his bodyguards literally blocked me in my seat and shielded the owner from even seeing me, a salty old sailor in faded clothes, who I'm sure they thought not worthy of his sight. I biked back to the boat in 40-mph winds as fast as I could, arriving to a white elephant sale sponsored by the RSR sailors.

On December 28th, a group of the RSR met by the Caltex fuel dock at 12:00 noon for a tour of the Port Ghalib complex. We were met by a German girl, who spoke passable English with a slight accent. We visited the hotel, which had 1100 rooms. Outside, It had the largest swimming pool in Egypt, and inside were many water displays, fountains, falls, etc. A room cost $200-300 USD per night, depending on the size and sea view. There were many bars in evidence at the complex. Also many restaurants, both fast foods like Pizza Hut, and sit-down, fancy, high-end restaurants in every one of the three hotels. The designer was from South Africa, with an Egyptian corporation. The money came from Kuwait and Saudi Arabia. We were shown a

Figure 43
Hotel Grounds

Figure 44

Hotel Rooms

Figure 45

Inside of the Hotel

Figure 46
Dining Room

Figure 47
Hotel Bar

Figure 48

Hotel Balcony

Figure 49

Hot Tub at Hotel

Figure 50
Marina Bar

large convention hall created for large and small groups, where it was hoped international conferences would take place. It was pointed out that only one road led to the complex, making it easy to establish security- monitoring points. We did not get to see the private airport, said to be the largest in Egypt. Later I joined Tim and Chris of "Reckless of Hamble" from England and Eva and Rolf of "Present" from Switzerland for a pizza and talk.

The next day the boys went to Aswan sightseeing and I went by bike to the north complex to send an e-mail but their service was down all day. The following day, the boys returned from Aswan where they had a good time sleeping on the ground some nights and in a hostel for 10 EGP ($1.85 USD) other nights. They had some problems getting there as all tourists are supposed to take a tour and join a convoy. They took a mini-van and were delayed at several checkpoints along the route to the dismay of the driver and his other passengers. A felucca captain had promised them a free ride in Lake Nasser, but he failed to show up. Talking with other people, they had received an invitation to a Nubian wedding. I was interested in finding out how it went and what they saw. It seemed to be common to invite foreigners to weddings as I had also attended them in other countries. It apparently gave the sponsors some prestige to have foreigners present.

On New Year's evening we had a dinner at the fancy marina restaurant, attended by about 20 RSR sailors, and had a wonderful time. The main thrill of the meal was the ostrich steak, which I had never eaten before. The "all you can eat" buffet was large with an extensive array of food and drink that was beyond imagination.

Figure 51

New Year's Decorations

Following the dinner, we retired to the pub where many Egyptians had already gathered. Nadia, from the RSR boat, "Alondra", provided singing and guitar playing, followed by belly dancers and various other acts, including the "Whirling Dervishes". Then, everyone began to dance, especially the Egyptians and their children, while wild Arabic music was played. It was a fun night and I will always remember it.

On Friday, January 4th, we sailed from Port Ghalib, Egypt, all the way to the Marsa Halaib anchorage, which is located in a large bay with only camels and a fisherman's shack for facilities. This is the center of the disputed "Halaib Triangle", which is land claimed by both Egypt and Sudan. The boundary between the two countries here was being determined by the international courts. Egypt had expelled the Sudanese and occupied the land. It was heavily fortified inland by an army base and at the marsa by a Navy ship. In the Red Sea, it's important to steer clear of the border areas as they are disputed and highly patrolled. We had been warned not to go there, but after three days at sea we needed to rest and repair our mainsail.

We were under sail most of the trip for 58 hours and covered over 290 miles south. We stood watch for two hours on and four hours off which seemed to work out fine for everyone except me. I had to keep a constant watch on our progress, checking the GPS frequently, and marking the chart. We continued this for three days and two nights. It turned into a tiring, but rewarding, trip. During one unusual gust of wind, the boys allowed the mainsail to jibe, ripping the sail in two places. Later in a harbor, we sewed it back together.

After anchoring for an hour or so in the marsa, we were visited by the Egyptian Navy personnel, who rowed out in a large rowboat and asked us to move up near their patrol boat for security reasons. We spent the night there peacefully, enjoying calm seas and no wind. For the first time this year, we received a light misty rain that muddied the deck and sails, which had been covered with dust and sand.

While motoring into the port, the engine had stopped and I had assumed it was the old problem of the fuel pump filter being plugged with algae, but after disassembling it the next day, I found that not to be the problem. Instead, I found the engine fuel filter full of water, dirt, and gunk. Putting on a new filter solved that problem. While I was working on this, I decided to replace the sacrificial zinc in the heat exchanger, but I was unable to remove the old one from its cap to put in a new one. Wanting an excuse for using the military harbor, I told the naval patrol boat about the problem. The Navy Captain came on board and convinced me to let them remove it and take it to the navy patrol boat to fix it.

I awoke the following day to a windy, stormy-looking sky. As we went further south, the days got less sunny and cloudier with even a little sprinkling of rain at times. The Egyptian naval patrol boat was just off our bow. We enjoyed being there and having their help and company. In return, we entertained them. They were very interested in us, as very few other boaters dare enter the military harbor and they are left alone for months on end. Yesterday the captain invited me to make a social call on board for tea and cookies. None of the sailors wore uniforms, just civilian clothes.

Figure 52
Navy Ship at Halaib

Ahmed, one of the sailors, told me I should try fishing, but I told him I didn't have any bait. He dipped into the patrol boat's freezer and came up with a fish that looked good enough to eat. He instructed me to use it as cut bait. I tried my luck without success but I watched him pull in fish off the patrol boat.

One morning when I came on deck I looked out and could not believe my eyes. A large herd of camels was grazing along the shore. Cows, calves, and bulls were peacefully eating bushes on the shore. I tried to take a picture, but I think they were too far away for a good picture. We began the repair of the ripped sails that morning. I have bad eyes and a low frustration point, so the job went frustratingly slowly. We finished half the job and planned to finish the rest the next day. I tried fishing again, but without any luck, so we had spaghetti that night for dinner. The next day, we sewed some more on the ripped mainsail. Later in the day, we explored the desert anchorage with the dinghy and did some fishing.

A strange thing happened with the instruments; the battery voltage and tachometer readings were going up and down but not the rpm of the motor itself. I found the drive belt to be slipping, causing the odd behavior. I installed a spare I had on hand and the problem was solved. We noticed that the farther south we went, the more storm clouds we saw. The deck was soaking wet this morning when we got up. It certainly looked like rain and a few drops even came down that day. The wind was increasing and was at gale force.

Naval Force-Egyptian Navy Patrol Boat No.11 was very helpful in the emergency repair of "Idyllic" in Halaib Harbor.

Figure 53
Sewing "Idyllic's" sail

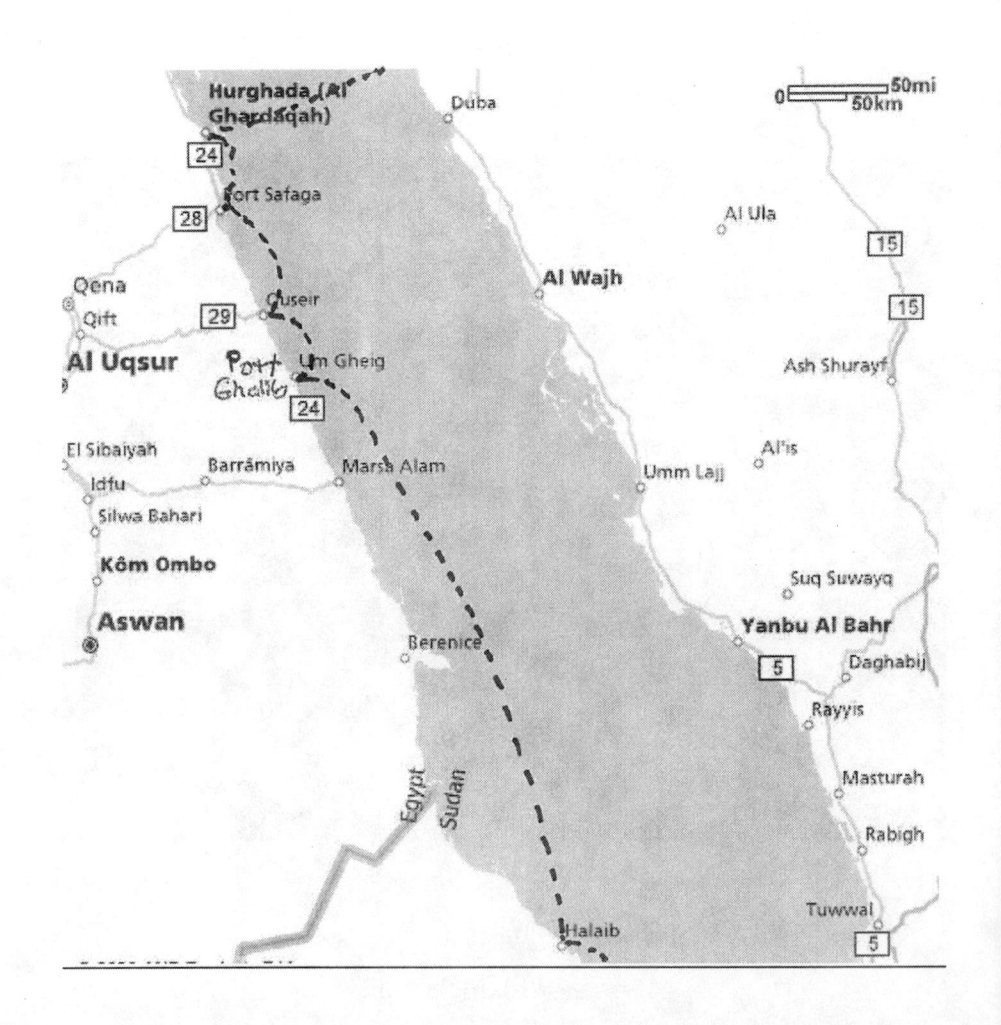

Figure 54
Route from Safaga, Egypt, to Marsa Oseif, Sudan

Especially helpful were Captain Shady Mohamed, Officer Mahmoud Tawfik, and Sailor Ahmed. These are great men and were wonderfully helpful and refused any money. They are an honor to Egypt.

Oseif, Sudan, to Massawa, Eritrea

On January 8th, we sailed for Oseif, Sudan. Elba Reef was a major challenge when we came down from the North. It was large and dangerous. With high seas, it was completely invisible, although it was on the charts and the GPS position was said to be accurate. We sweated, fussed, and checked the waypoints repeatedly as we got closer. Holding our breath, we were sure we were on the right heading when finally it became visible. We were past it and on the southern side! Up until this time, it was completely invisible. Even the wave action and the normal color changes of the water over a reef were masked and of no help.

We were under sail the entire trip to Khor Abu Asal at Marsa Oseif. We had intended to go to a different port, but we couldn't find the entrance to that port due to its small size and lack of features. So we settled for Oseif, which had two radio masts and two large fuel tanks to help us identify the small opening to the bay. We motored near to a jetty where a man was standing and asked him if we could come alongside. He waved us on into the anchorage.

Osief is a town, if you want to call it that. It was a collection of huts that we later found to be a refugee camp filled with Christians expelled from Halaib by the Egyptians. Along the bay, there were about ten small shacks on stilts that the people used as outhouses, which somewhat discouraged us from swimming. There were no sewage facilities, no water pipes, and no electricity. After dark,

Figure 55
"Idyllic" Sailing

Figure 56

Harold at the Helm

Figure 57

Anchoring "Idyllic"

there were several thousand people without one electric light. It was an unbelievably quiet night with no wind or waves. There was no sound except for donkeys braying, dogs barking, and roosters crowing. When I checked the anchor at 4:00 a.m., the only light showing was the red light on the top of the radio tower.

We sailed that morning and on January 10th, arrived at the Khor Shinab anchorage. This was a beautiful marsa anchorage like those shown in dream pictures, almost six miles deep into the great western desert with mountains, plains, and beautiful scenery. Seven boats of the RSR were there and the next morning several left, going south.

I radioed in ahead and was immediately invited to a fish BBQ on shore. We brought our appetites, a can of corn, and a can of carrots to heat over the wood fire. Only two fish, called blue tang, had been caught that day, but they were large. In addition, there was one large tuna from the previous day's catch, so there was plenty for everyone. They were cooked over a wood fire and were delicious. Others brought casseroles of rice, beans, meat, and mushrooms. We also ate a cabbage salad that was delicious. In our excitement we forgot to bring plates so we ate on pot tops and with our fingers. I drank wine out of an empty corn can. I was given an update on the election news in the USA and news of the RSR participants. This anchorage was empty, without any people, lights, or noise - just mountains, flats, and desert. Right at sunset the boys climbed Quoin Hill, which gave them an awe-inspiring view of the far-off mountains and desert.

Figure 58
Khor Shinab

On January 11th, we arrived at Wreck Recovery Anchorage. This was a reef-strewn bay, to which we could not find an entrance. We found out later that the rest of the boats had passed it up as too difficult, and went on to Mohammed Kohl instead. Large waves were breaking all around us making for a dangerous anchorage that was noisy and unsafe. We finally found a very small area of not very smooth water, with a 25-foot depth, behind the reef. It appeared to be high tide and we hoped, when the tide receded, the breaking waves would die down. The wind usually died down at night, which would help calm the waves down or else we were in for a bumpy night. Joe prepared a special meal of meat and potatoes for me. He and Nico were vegetarians and did not eat meat.

The next morning, we had an hour's struggle to extract the anchor from the clutches of the reef. As it was, we lost the small mushroom anchor we use as a weight. I felt we were lucky to get out that easy, as it was a difficult situation without any room to maneuver, having reefs on all sides with only a small opening out.

We sailed to Marsa Salak that day. Coming into the harbor, we were worried about the shallow water that was only two meters deep, but it turned out not to be a problem as tides in the Red Sea were negligible. A large school of manta rays was swimming about at the entrance, surfacing and feeding. We found the "Mylias", a catamaran from France, in the harbor. We had seen their mast while still at sea.

When the Egyptian navy cleaned my heat exchanger, they must have made a hole in it, as I discovered I had some salt water mixed

Figure 59
Marsa Salak

into the fresh water tank, which was not good. I thought perhaps I could get it fixed at Suakin. I was sure looking forward to a break from sailing. I was getting tired after 800 miles of fast, downwind sailing with large waves. Thank goodness for the boys' help, which was invaluable.

Ghee from the "Mylias" came over that night and invited us to go back with him for a fish soup dinner. They had also invited John-Louis and Denise from the "Alero" of Montreal, Canada. They were great drinkers, so they had an inexhaustible supply of wine, whiskey, and beer to drink. They had a steering gear failure on the "Mylias", which Ghee had spent hours trying to solve after sailing all night with an emergency tiller. Finally after fixing it in a creative way, Ghee found he had installed the gears backwards so that when he turned right, the boat turned left and vise versa. This would have made an interesting day of reverse sailing if he had not checked it out before leaving. "Alero" had gone on a reef and required other boats to pull her off. That story had a happy ending. Everyone spoke and understood French, so talk was going a mile a minute with me trying to understand some of it, as my French is meager. Denise was sober, so she tried to translate for me, which was appreciated. A good time was had by all and Ghee transported us back to "Idyllic" in his dinghy.

We sailed 30 miles to Marsa Fijab the next day without any problems. At Marsa Fijab, my bilge pump didn't work and had refused to work for the past two days. I thought the wiring had become disconnected, but after working in the oily water in the bilge, I found the outlet pipe had become disconnected. Nico saved the day by

Figure 60
Marsa Fijab

Figure 61

Camels Carrying Firewood

Figure 62

Charcoal Factory

hanging upside down and reattaching it. After reconnecting, it worked fine, thank goodness!

Bad news was received that day. The "Panta Rhei" had hit a reef called Shab Rumi and the captain and crew were fortunately saved by a dive boat that was anchored on the reef. The Captain of the Panta Rhei saw the reef at the last moment and sheared off, but the boat hit the reef, tearing off the keel and washing progressively farther up with every wave. "Alondra" and "Mistral" are leaving tonight to try to help and to pick up the survivors from the dive boat by the reef. They will try to save as much equipment and supplies as possible.

"Panta Rhei" had set off their EPR when they went on the reef. The signal was picked up by the Dutch Coast Guard, who called their reference, Willem's son, who called the RSR, who investigated and found them shipwrecked. The Sudanese agent and police made a report and said everything was OK, but later the police wanted to take Willem to the wreck to investigate before he left the country. The net result was that the insurance company had to pay 25,000 EUR ($38,665 USD) for damage to the reefs.

On January 14th, we entered Marsa Darar, a marsa with land far away and only the reef to protect us from the large ocean waves. The wind was howling at 50 knots and a bit of swell was reaching the inner area of the open anchorage, but the anchor held well. The water was brown with silt from inland rains, which had made the bay very shallow. We anchored in about seven feet of water. The sun was very hot and we appreciated the strong wind that allowed us to breathe.

On the way into port, I tried fishing and immediately hooked a tuna. He was much too big, as we were traveling 6-7 knots, and he broke off. An hour later, I hooked a smaller tuna, which we ate that night. In the harbor, there were about 50 manta rays playing around the boat and as far as the eye could see. Never had I seen so many in one place. Several Sudanese fishermen were there and one boat wanted to sell us 2 eggs for 10 SDG ($5.00 USD). They must have come from golden hens. We were told that the Sudanese large fishing boats had all been burned, as a result of the smuggling with Saudi Arabia, so all of the fishing boats were small open boats with outboard motors.

I had trouble getting the boys up the next morning, although we had planned to leave at first light with "Mylias". "Mylias" had trouble starting their port engine before we left. We entered Port Suakin harbor on January 15th and called port control. They wanted my name and the name of the boat, which I kept repeating over and over for him, finally spelling everything out. He kept getting it wrong and I soon gave up. I finally considered changing my name to Mohamed. Suakin, Sudan, was the last slave-trading city in the world, stopping only after WWII ended.

It was certainly a good feeling to be in port to work on the engine problems, travel to Bur Sudan to shop, resupply, and e-mail home. I went ashore the next day and met Mohammed, Agent for Sudan, who gave me three shore passes in exchange for our passports. He also exchanged $100 for 200 SDG (Sudanese pounds). I arranged

Figure 63

Mohammed, Agent for Sudan, with Harold

to pick up water and fuel later in the week. My expenses paid to Mohammed at Suakin were as follows:

Port Fee	$ 20
Customs	20
30X3 Immigration Fee	90
Agents fee	30
Fuel+water	<u>161</u>
Total	$ 321

The ruins of a beautiful city, once made entirely of coral, were all around the north shore. All that remained were piles of rubble and half-destroyed buildings, hotels, churches, stores, residences, and slave markets. Sudan's wars with Egypt and others for independence all caused massive damage to the entire city.

I worked most of the day trying to find the leak of salt water into the freshwater side of the engine. I finally found the hole in the heat exchanger and Rene from "Alondra" said he knew how to fix the problem. I was concerned, as the time in Suakin was running out before the RSR continued.

On January 18th there was a general meeting of all the RSR sailors. Lo, the Director of the RSR, reported the "Panta Rhei" was high on the reef and would soon break up while the fishermen and divers were stripping her of everything of value. They had been sailing from Inkafel to Sauganey Reef and hit the Shab Rumi Reef, believing they were several miles away. They did not realize they were off course. It was a terrible miscalculation and we had to make sure we didn't do the same. We planned to increase our fixes to several each

Figure 64

Lo, RSR Organizer, from Mistral

Figure 65
Panta Rhei On a Reef

hour, and every few minutes when in the area of reefs. The Red Sea Guide recommends steering three miles clear of reefs during the day and five miles at night. "Tardy" had struck a reef near where "Panta Rhei" had struck the Shab Rumi Reef.

Lo insisted that all radio transmission on channel 77 by RSR boats be in English so everyone could understand. We were to use other channels to speak in other languages. We had crews that spoke French, English, Dutch, and German. Some had problems speaking and understanding English. Lo pointed out that if you risk the safety of your own boat, you also risk the safety of other boats. Some boats had been giving information on their websites causing problems. Lo asked everybody to clear information through him first before publishing it on a website. Lo warned us that, because of Eritrea's continuing war with Ethiopia, the government had placed severe restrictions on diesel fuel and that it would not be possible to buy fuel in Eritrea. He recommended that we fill up our tanks before leaving Sudan.

The RSR chartered a bus to Port Sudan for a one-day visit. The trip through the desert was unforgettable. We saw mile after mile of Bedouin villages with wooden and tent homes. There were camels, goats, and donkeys everywhere, shepherded by women and children standing guard. How people can survive in such extreme conditions is hard to understand, but they have done so throughout the ages.

As we entered Port Sudan, I saw tremendously large trucking firms with hundred of oilrigs and oil trucks parked in large guarded

Figure 66

Road from Suakin to Port Sudan

Figure 67

Market in Port Sudan

Figure 68

Tour Guide with Eva and Rolf from "Present"

Figure 69

Ras & Jerry from "Mandarina"

Figure 70

Rolf behind Eva with Ras

Figure 71

Marijke from "Sepia"

areas enclosed by fences. We found Lo, with "Mistral", in the port and he gave us detailed instructions on how to find an e-mail café and souks (markets). I first tried e-mailing, but the café lost power and I had to give up. I went to a large supermarket that was only the size of a small grocery in the United States. Then I rode a tuk-tuk (motorized rickshaw) carrying two large bags of groceries, back to our charter bus. We planned to buy fresh fruits and vegetables back closer to the boat.

On the night of the 18th, I visited Sharon and John on "Dionysus" to see if they could charge my mobile VHF battery. They were from America and had a 110v generator on their boat. They later returned my mobile VHF battery fully charged.

On the 19th, I went into the city of Suakin with my camera to take some pictures and go shopping for a v-belt for the engine. I took a walk through the town and it was interesting to see the many destroyed buildings. The ones in use were in terrible repair; we would call them shacks. The main street was dirt, dusty, and full of ruts. Donkey carts hauling people and produce were everywhere. Three wheeled tuk-tuks were used as taxis, with only a few larger taxis in evidence. I estimated the number of them at about one per thousand people. Small mini-van buses were available and, at a bus station, large buses to other cities were available.

I had received e-mail messages but had not been able to respond, as computer use was unbelievably slow and expensive. We planned to leave soon for Massawa, Eritrea, 450 miles south. The time for leaving port had been advanced, as the conditions for sailing were

Figure 72
Tuk Tuk

poor and the longer we waited, the more unreliable the north winds were becoming. The weather had become calmer and the high waves and winds were subsiding. We would soon hit contrary south winds for the first time that would require us to motor more often.

We left Suakin late on January 19th and picked up high winds during the night that became somewhat more modest during the next day. The weather was cloudy with just little bit of rain. As we sailed out of the harbor, I got wet from the waist down as a large wave swept over the side of the cockpit. We sailed the whole way with good winds from the north. The boys both seemed to be a little under the weather. They blamed it on eating some dates I bought that had insects inside. We arrived safely at the Trinkitat harbor anchorage after a full day's sail in high winds and waves. We anchored in 10 feet of water with a nasty swell running. I hoped the winds and swell would die during the evening.

Trinkitat, Sudan, was very primitive with many donkey carts and herds of camels about. The people were wonderful, but dirt poor. Their homes were of sticks, skins, tin, and pieces of wood washed up from the sea. Fortunately the weather was hot with little or no rain even in the wet season or winter.

"Idyllic" was beginning to show her age with repaired sails, plugged heat exchanger, a leaking exhaust, and a broken water pump. These were small problems when compared to other boats that had been forced to drop out with major problems. There were 14 boats left, out of the 41 that had started. Some had planned to stop along the way and return north. I had made some great friends, who had been very kind and helpful, especially during emergencies. The crew, Joe and Nico, were great and helped more every day that passed, as they learned more about sailing, navigation, and boat repair.

When sailing south from Trinkitat, we ran into south winds about 20 miles out and had to return to the Trinkitat anchorage. The engine had started overheating and I could not find the problem. A friend promised to come and try to find the answer to the problem at 9:00 a.m. the next morning. I was afraid I would not be able to continue on until the trouble was fixed. Between the dangerous reefs and the motor not running properly, the situation was becoming depressing. The difficult sailing and the isolation of the country was pushing me to the limit. I was beginning to have second thoughts about continuing.

On January 26th we left Trinkitat Harbor with high hopes of sailing to Massawa in Eritrea. This was not to be. The wind changed to the southeast and then died completely. We drifted all night, circling around and around with the currents. There was quite a swell running that made things creak and bang about on board. Early light found a fresh breeze out of the west and our hopes went up, as the breeze freshened. But four miles later, a dead calm settled in again. With no engine there was no movement, except for the leftover swell. The last 380 miles promised to be a lengthy transit.

Later the wind picked up considerably and we were off to the south on course. Joe had a seagull sit on his shoulder, tame as could be. We were thankful that "Alero", the French-Canadian boat from Quebec with John-Louis and Denise on board, kept us company and left their light on so we could follow in the dark without our instruments running our batteries down. What a rush, to sail 400 miles without an engine, in reef strewn seas, knowing only the wind is there to help! For three days and three nights we continued our journey, starting with no wind and calm seas for a whole night, changing to light winds, and finally developing into a tremendous northern storm with black skies enveloping the entire northern horizon and then "Idyllic" herself in a fury of wind, rain, and incredible seas. Fortunately, this was from the north, so that we could easily run with the wild wind, high waves, and seas, which were beyond imagination. For 50 miles, we traveled at well over 5 knots without any sails, driven by the high winds gusting to 50 knots or higher, as we continually reefed them down to bare poles. The storm raged on with rain and wind so furious that the seagulls took refuge on board; not one, but several at a time. On another boat one even came on board and died. One poor fellow came on board and landed on the rail behind me after I took over the helm from Joe. I reached up and slid my finger under him and lifted him onto the seat next to me. He rested there for an hour, until I accidentally piled the flopping jib sheet right on top of him. He put up an awful shriek until I dug him out from under the pile, but he refused to leave and stayed the rest of the trip. Sometimes I reached down to pet him and he made no protest. This even seemed like a comfort to him.

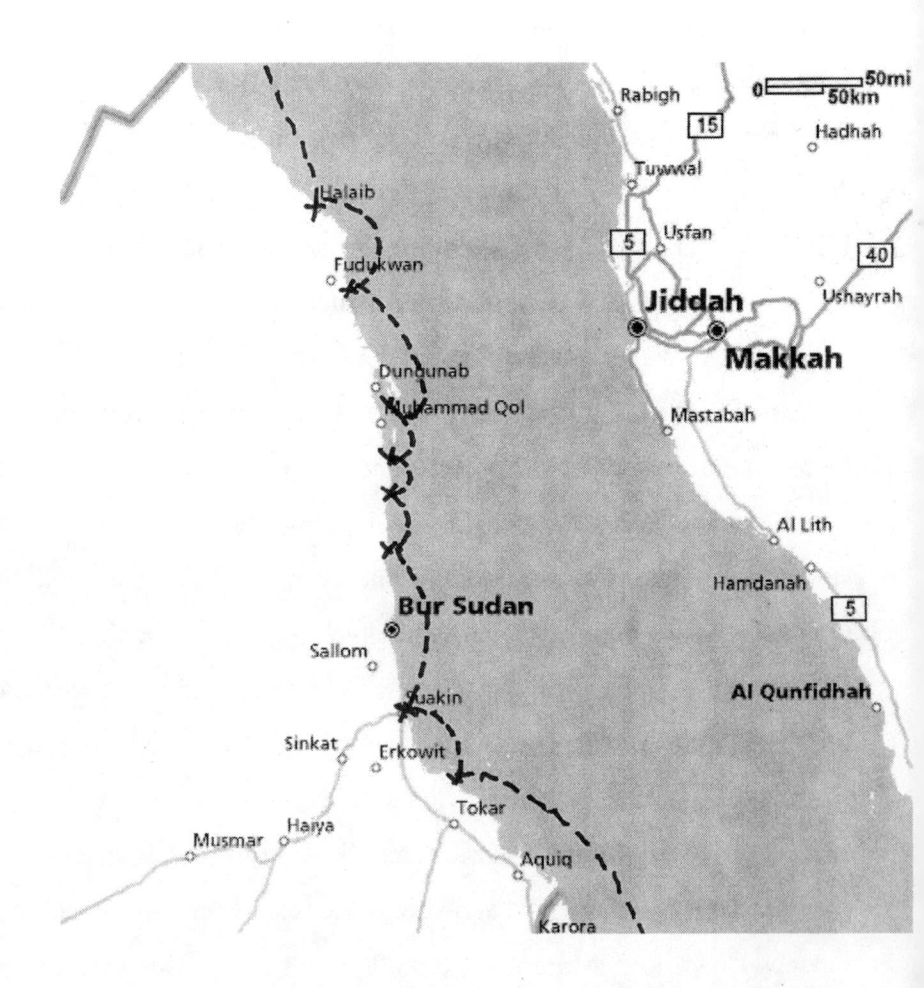

Figure 73

Route from Marsa Halaib, Sudan, to Trinkitat, Sudan

Massawa, Eritrea to Asmara, Eritrea

As we approached Massawa, we found we were far too early, so we loitered the last 10 miles calling on the VHF for guidance to the anchorage. We had followed "Alero"'s light all night and were in frequent radio contact with them, which was a real blessing and gave us much confidence. The wind was contrary to the anchorage and Rene, from "Alondra", came out in the foul weather to offer assistance when we ran a line from "Alero" to pull us into port. I had intended to go to Customs and Immigration right away, but was told the office was closed. I was relieved not to have to take the dinghy out in the rain to the dock.

I took the freshwater pump off the engine that morning and a fellow named Captain Jack from the "Miss Cat" promised to take me to a mechanic to have it fixed. Also, the water box needed welding where the exhaust and water mix. We planned to stay in Massawa only about a week, so I was hoping I wouldn't have to wait for parts. I wanted to leave there with my RSR friends. Jack picked me up and took me to the port where he introduced me to the Chief Engineer of "Arlus", a big tugboat, and Ibraham, a mechanic, who said he would be willing to work on the parts.

At 9:00 a.m., I received a call that the mechanic wanted to see me and talk about the problems. But first I had to go to Customs and Immigration, the Harbormaster, the bank, the harbor cashier, and the

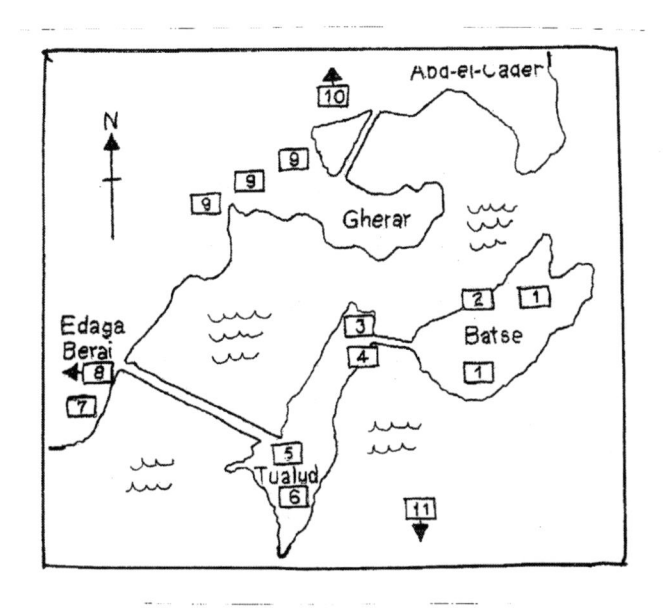

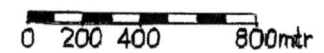

[1] Old Town
[2] Dockyards / Port
[3] Gibi (Imperial palace)
[4] Dahlak and Central Hotel
[5] War Monument
[6] Red Sea Hotel
[7] Massawa Housing Complex
[8] (to) Massawa Bus Terminal
[9] Salt Ponds
[10] (to) Gurgussum Beach (hotels)
[11] (to) Green Island

Figure 74

Massawa Harbor

Figure 75

Docks at Massawa

Figure 76

Savoya Hotel on Dock at Massawa

Figure 77

Entrance to Savoya Hotel

Figure 78

Central Square, Batse Island

Figure 79

Bar on Batse Island

Figure 80

Old Architecture, Old Town Massawa

Figure 81

Mosque on Batse Island

Figure 82

Causeway from Batse Island to Massawa

visa office to log in to Eritrea. Finally my papers and reports were in order, stamped and approved. By then, it was late in the afternoon and I was tired. I went back to the boat, had some soup, and rested. That night I visited "Alondra" where we looked at my pictures and theirs of our travels so far, after which they served me dinner. I made a CD of "Idyllic" sailing videos and photos that they had taken during the trip.

On January 30th we were still working on the water pump problem. Some mechanics in Massawa thought they could repair it. There weren't any parts in town, so I would have to go to Asmara, the capital of Eritrea, to find what I needed.

I was impressed by the cleanliness of the streets and homes in Massawa,. They made a real effort to keep things clean. I went to the New Massawa City to shop for groceries and found it to be a shantytown of corrugated tin and wood shacks with extremely poor people, but still clean. In some areas, new buildings were being started and a few were even occupied before being finished. I got a haircut for one dollar US and tea for a nickel. All prices were very cheap. For the first time, I was able to e-mail, but soon the power went out and put a stop to that again.

In Eritrea, the Government has outlawed plastic bags. I found this out the hard way by placing my trash in a plastic bag on the Government Port Pier of Massawa where I had moored the "Idyllic". Someone banging on the hull brought me on deck in a hurry to face a bent old lady wearing an orange striped vest. She unloaded a string of adjectives in Arabic, which I didn't understand until she took me roughly by one hand and, with my trash bags in the other hand, marched us to a hidden, truck trash-receptacle. After she shook her finger in my face, I realized I had committed a serious offence. When I asked an English-speaking local I found that the woman had been very concerned that the police, who were within 50 feet of my boat guarding the entrance gate and watching my every move, would arrest me.

In my travels, I find I never go far without seeing a discarded plastic bag. Researching this, I discovered the worldwide demand for plastic bags is 50 billion a year. When trolling the waters off the west coast of Italy, I found it difficult to fish, as I kept hooking plastic bags. When diving in Turkey, I found the bottom almost covered with plastic. The fishermen there were complaining about the lack of fish in the past few years. I believe this is related.

Plastic bags are handy and lightweight; however, they are made out of oil that is becoming expensive and in short supply. The main problem is they take hundreds of years to degrade, if ever. Paper bags were used in the past. Paper self-destructs when it gets wet or exposed to the sun, but paper is made from trees and its manufacture creates air and water pollution. In a lot of countries, cloth bags have become popular, as they are reusable.

San Francisco, Oakland, China, and Eritrea have banned plastic bags. McDonald's, facing public pressure, has done away with plastic hamburger boxes and switched to paper, thus gaining a lot of goodwill. In my opinion, the U.S. should ban plastic bags.

Figure 83

Imperial Palace, Tualud Island

Figure 84

Dahlak Hotel, Tualud Island

Figure 85

Massawa Minibus to Asmara

Shopping for supplies in town was fun. If you needed meat, you could have them chop off a chunk, after chasing the flies off, at the local grocery shop or you can go to the goat salesman with a flock on the corner, pick out a good looking goat to purchase, lead him home, and butcher it yourself for good fresh meat. Cows were bought at a market outside of town, butchered out on the desert, and divided up among several families. Needless to say, my consumption of red meat decreased significantly and my crew refused to eat any red meat.

After applying for a "Foreign Visitors Permit to Travel" and receiving the permit on January 31st, I had to wait two days for the Security office to see me and stamp my permit. I finally left "Idyllic" and Massawa on February 2nd to travel to Asmara and after all this, no one even asked to see the permit at the checkpoints along the way. Asmara, the capital of Eritrea, is a beautiful, cool, tree-lined city, high up in the mountains at 6,000 feet elevation. It was a pleasant place to visit. The climb up to it by highway is spectacular, with scenery at every turn, and there are hundreds of turns with people and animals at every other turn. Camels, goats, sheep, baboons, cows, and hundreds of people use the highway as a trail to their villages and pastures. Farms along the way were growing corn, potatoes, tomatoes, tea, citrus fruits, and vegetables of all kinds. Old tanks **and** destroyed military vehicles from past wars dotted the roadside.

Upon arriving in Asmara, I checked into the African Pension, an old, but comfortable and well-run hotel, at a cost of 130 ERN (Eritrean nakfa) or $8.70 USD a night. My room was a separate room in the back of the hotel, probably made for workers to use. One light, one sink, and one single bed, spartan but clean and quiet. Stage 3 they called it.

One of the highlights of the trip was a visit to the military cemetery, again requiring one permit to visit and another to photograph. Not an ordinary cemetery but a cemetery of military vehicles from the war of independence. There were tanks, personnel carriers, Jeeps, and all kinds of hardware, along with the ammunition for the guns. Mostly Russian, but some American, all given to Ethiopia to use in its war to occupy Eritrea. We climbed and scrambled about the equipment to the consternation of our security guides who gave up trying to corral us. Climbing inside the American tank to look at the motors, installed in the Muskegon factory a few miles from my home, I raised and lowered the large guns, sat in the driver's seat, and thoroughly enjoyed myself. Ammunition and guns were lying all about. Airplanes, that had been destroyed at the airport, were also there in jumbled piles. Interestingly, old American antique cars were parked there in rows along with discarded buses and taxis.

On February 4th, back in Massawa, we went to the copy shop across town, but they were closed. We had been misinformed that they opened at 8:00 a.m.. Joe stayed to copy the charts, while I went to the port to meet the chief engineer and give him the motor repair parts I brought from Asmara. He was waiting for me on the tug, "Arlus". He immediately took the parts to the machinists, who went right to work and had the pump reassembled by 9:00 a.m.. I could not find Joe, who was supposed to be waiting for me. I looked all around for him in the

Figure 86

Oldest Part of Massawa

Figure 87

Post Office, Massawa

Figure 88

Public Library, Massawa

Figure 89

Railway Station, Massawa

Figure 90

St. Mary's Church, Massawa

Figure 91

Commercial Bank of Eritrea, Massawa

port and town, but could not find him, so I returned to "Idyllic" and started the process of installing the water pump on the engine. This was soon accomplished. I ran the engine to test it and found it ran cool and correctly.

Now that the engine was repaired, the winds that were from the north for a week had turned to the south, keeping us in port and making southern progress almost impossible. The south winds had arrived, humid, sticky, and hot. This was expected to continue for the next six days. I planned to enjoy the next day on shore shopping, looking around, and getting ready to leave.

I spent part of the morning visiting John and Sharon on "Dionysis". A part of the time we spent assembling our newly copied charts. It took eight pages per chart and the two of us took a long time getting them taped together in some sort of order. I finally learned the name for the large unusual looking birds that land on the fishing boat next to us. According to Sharon they are spoon-billed storks.

We moved to the pier on Wednesday, February 6th, in order to prepare to leave. I bought water, fruit, and veggies in the old town, but missed checking out with customs before 12:00 noon, so I planned to leave the next morning at 7:00 a.m. We had a full load of water and fuel, so we were prepared. It was depressing sitting in port, unable to leave because of the south wind stopping us. I'm beginning to have more stress than ever before trying to cope with all of the problems. That night the wind went calm and then switched to the north.

On February 7th, we left and then returned to the pier after a few miles. I had left Massawa with high hopes, but the motor had

Figure 92

Hotel Torino

Figure 93

Massawa Woman Boiling Coffee

Figure 94

Saba, Bartender at Kokhab Bar, Massawa

overheated again and forced me to return to port. Ibraham agreed to try to fix the problem when he got off work at 2:00 p.m. I was beside myself with frustration.

The next day, Ibraham, the port mechanic, worked on the overheating problem for three hours without success. I thought I found the problem myself that morning. The saltwater mixer was still not working. I decided there must be crud somewhere inside, stopping the water flow. I ran a hose outside and as soon as I did, the engine ran cool. So I decided that must be the problem. I decided I had to find a new mixer, which would be hard to do.

The next day I still didn't have a solution to the engine-overheating problem. I decided to go to the Ship Repair Yard for help. I had spent 16 days in Massawa so far and it appeared that I would have to spend more time. My crew kept my spirits up with jokes and encouragement. There wasn't any talk of their leaving, only sticking it out and helping any way they could. Soon all the RSR boats would be gone and we would have the problem of being alone on our own to fend for ourselves.

I spent the next morning cleaning the heat exchanger with Clorox bleach. The Egyptian cleaned it with acid, but forgot there were two sides and they missed one side and it was full of rust and junk. I took out the thermostat to see if that was the problem. I ran the engine when it was back together and it stayed cool for over two hours. On to Yemen! Hurray! I reinstalled the thermostat and everything seemed to be fine.

Figure 95
Nico with Barracuda

On Februrary 12th, we again left the Massawa Port pier. By now I was not checking in and out, at each office, which took a minimum of a half-day's paperwork for nothing. We motored the first day and night with a light north wind pushing us along. We were sailing with "Reckless of Hamble", "Dionysus", and "Alero". Soon these larger boats began to pass us as they were going full speed to make up time. In the dark, their lights soon disappeared. For 24 hours, we didn't see a soul except for the lights of fishing boats over by Saudi Arabia. One came at us at full speed, full of rough looking characters in a long, old-looking boat pushed by an outboard motor. They asked, by gestures, for cigarettes, which we didn't have. In the boat were two large hammerhead sharks, which they had caught. These sharks filled the boat and required the fishermen to stand on the seats, out of the way. After they left, the smell was still quite noticeable, but the threat of piracy left with them.

We motored south for a day and a night from Massawa, halfway to Assab. Then the fresh water pump bearing failed, so we sailed 30 miles back to Anfil Bay during the night, arriving at 7:00 a.m. on February 14th. We anchored in 10 feet of water behind Haunt Deset Island. It was a very good anchorage, behind the island and well sheltered from the 35-knot winds out of the south. Between the island and the reef the waves are almost nonexistent. It was deserted and I didn't know how long I would have to stay there, so the boys decided to give up and try to get to Aden. Out of the 41 boats that started in the RSR, there were only 13 left to continue.

What a fix! I couldn't believe I was in such a fix. Here I was in a primitive area without transportation. I could sail, but it would be a dangerous risk with the unpredictable winds coming first from the north and then the south, especially single-handed. I was hoping some fishermen would come along and give us a ride to shore, but no one came. This was a desolate place with only pink storks and giant pelicans to keep us company. The anchorage was very protected, but far from land.

On Saturday, the 16th I awoke, with hope and enthusiasm, to the sound of an outboard motor. Scrambling into the cockpit, I saw a fishing boat across the bay a few miles away. After yelling and fruitlessly waving, I dug out the 12-gage aerial flare gun and set off a red flare. It was impressive, but unseen, as the fast boat continued on its way, giving us a feeling of hopelessness. An hour later, a small boat with three fishermen on board came directly toward the island. Again, all three of us waved and hollered. They seemed to have seen us, but due to the reef, headed away from our location. They soon resumed a course toward us. The closer they came, the harder we waved. When they arrived at the boat, we explained in gestures, English, and as much Arabic as we could muster, that we needed a ride to shore. They said "Thio" (the name of a nearby village) several times and asked how much. We offered money, "Nakfa," but they kept saying, "Benzene". They needed gasoline for their outboard. I took out our outboard gas tank and gave it to them with the funnel. After pouring the gas into their can, they said OK to get in.

Then followed a mad scramble to gather up our belongings for the trip, not knowing when we could come back. I forgot a coat, but the boys were all prepared with big backpacks containing all their earthly possessions. We jumped into the large fishing boat with all of our bags and headed off across the reef for the shore. It was low tide, so we took a circuitous route through the reef with a lookout on the bow to help steer. Soon we were clear and at full speed, heading in the direction of shore.

Soon, another boat showed up with two boys in it and our fishermen flagged it down. After a long discussion, they indicated they wanted us to get in that boat with the permission of the two boys, who were laughing and happy. We complied because we didn't really have a choice. Off we headed again in a slightly different direction, more south than before. But they soon ran out of gas. What they were doing without gas way out in the ocean is a good question; however, the boys were only amused and fished out a long pole and started poling the boat. The first boat, seeing the boys poling, came back and, after I reminded them that I had given them benzene to take us to shore, they gave us back some gas so we could get to shore.

We barely made it, as the gas in the tank was so bad, it was hardly able to keep the engine running. It was actually stopping at times. We landed on a beach where there was a gathering of many fishermen on a sand bank protruding out into the sea. Behind the fishermen were a dozen primitive stick, hide-covered homes. I was approached by their chief, who spoke some English. He asked what we wanted and if he could help. We told him we needed to go to town

Figure 96

Nico and Joe with Fishermen

Figure 97
Anfil Bay Fisherman

Figure 98

Drying the Nets

for motor parts. This request brought on a lot of discussion among the fishermen and they ran to get another fisherman who was working on his boat down the beach. They said they would take us to town for 600 ERN. After some negotiation, we settled on 300 ERN ($20 USD). I arranged for one of the fishermen to guard the "Idyllic" while I was gone.

Apparently the trip to Thio was a big deal, because the fishermen scurried off and returned with a jerry can, bags of fish, and who knows what else. Several of them immediately launched the boat, which by then was high and dry, as the tide had gone out. We jumped in with their belongings and with ours, pretty well filling the boat. Off we went to the town of Thio. It turned into a long journey in the open sea, with waves washing over the gunnels, along with spray soaking everyone and everything on board. On the way, we hit some object and it sheared off the propeller shear pin. One of the fishermen crawled out onto the stern, unscrewed the nut holding the propeller, and inserted a piece of a screwdriver he had broken off as a substitute for the shear pin. It didn't work very well, but it did manage to get us to Thio, a distance of about 10 miles.

We arrived at the fishermen's cooperative and were led to the Navy Commander, who called a sailor over to translate for him. They were more than interested and called navy mechanics, who were sure they could fix the problem, saying, "No problem mon". With several bystanders and the entire Eritrea navy, they soon had the pump dismantled and in several pieces. The bearing was shot with the little steel balls worn and some even flat. They tried to find motor parts

Figure 99

Stick Homes

Figure 100

Thio Restaurant

Figure 101

Nico Buying Water that Turned Green

with ball bearings; a generator, an alternator, a bicycle wheel, and various other interesting looking machines, were all examined to no avail. Even the town's bicycle repair shop was called in with another bag of bearings that we put in and tried without success.

We decided we needed to get back to Massawa for a new bearing. The Commander said he would write a permit for us to travel. They then gave us a ride to the main highway where we could pick up a bus. After we arrived at the main highway, the bus came after only an hour's wait. It was full of baggage and people; tired one and all, as they had been riding for hours from Assab. We crowded on with our bags and were soon cleared by the army. Having the army pass speeded our clearance considerably. By the time we got started, it was dark and I anticipated a long sleep. However, that was not to be, as we were stopped about two miles out of town by a white pickup that someone said was security. The two buses turned around, unloaded everyone, and said they were going back to Assab in couple of hours. All of those people had ridden for eight hours, only to be told they would be returned to their starting point.

We went back out to the desert to pick a place to sleep. The boys didn't like the isolation, so we returned to town and found an old cattle corral where we lay down in the sheep manure, sticks, rocks, and unseen debris, soon falling asleep. It wasn't long before an army checkpoint guard came and asked what we were doing. I told him, "No money", which he seemed to understand, although the next day he politely showed us a hotel for $2 a bed.

Figure 102

Our Campsite

Figure 103

Joe and Nico in Restaurant

Figure 104

Bull in Restaurant

The next day, our newly made friends at a restaurant whispered that an army truck was arriving at 8:00 a.m. and we should be there. They offered to wake us up at 7:00 a.m. with breakfast at no charge. The whole time we were there, they would not take money for food, beds, or anything. When I asked why, they said, "You are strangers".

The next morning, a large, double-axle, army truck pulled up, laden with supplies and about 20 Arabs situated on top. Security gave them the once over, searched the truck inside and out, and proclaimed it safe to continue. All this time, I was asking for a ride and the price. The only answer I got was "not much", which made me real uneasy, as this is a favorite saying until you're hooked, and then it's astronomically high. We piled on by climbing a ladder. I had a difficult time of it with my pack. Someone said something and I was put in the front seat of the truck with the driver, the Commander, and another old man. This was a very tiring, eight-hour trip that included changing two flat tires along the way.

When we arrived at Massawa, we went to the Massawa Hotel to find a room. I tried to get a room for the three of us, but he wanted too much money. I asked why. For one it was 100 ERN but he would not allow us to rent for three. I persisted for an explanation and when Fathi, the hotel owner, saw I wouldn't give up, he patiently explained that it was against the law, but if I wanted two girls that would be fine, "No problem"!

I met with a couple of my friends, Moussi and Ben Zimmo, and we discussed my problems. They said they would help in any way they could. I called my wife, Vonda, and planned to have her get the

Figure 105

Army Truck to Massawa with Flat Tire

Figure 106

Joe and Nico on Top

Figure 107

My Front Seatmates

Figure 108
House on Road to Massawa

Figure 109

Ceremonial Coffee with Incense at Roadhouse

Figure 110
Second Flat Tire

Figure 111

Joe, Nico, and Harold in Massawa

parts I needed and ship them to my friend, Leslie, in the Netherlands. He could then ship them to me in Massawa.

Fathi needed to go to the capital, Asmara, where he had a house and offered to take me there the next day to try to get the parts. The next day, February 19th, Fathi was ready to go at about 9:00 a.m., but when he went to get fuel with his government permit, the gas station was out of fuel. They gave the usual answer, "Come back tomorrow". The next day, he filled up and off we went. He had a small Nissan van with rather poor tires, loaded down with grain, salt, and sugar in big sacks in the back.

The first part of the trip was through the desert where we saw sheep, goats, and camels with shepherds in abundance. There were small Bedouin villages along the road, where there were many people trying to get a ride. Fathi passed all of them without picking anyone up. Soon we started to climb a road with many switchbacks and with increasingly steep grades. It was necessary to honk on the turns as we used the entire road to make the sharp turns and if a truck was coming it needed even more room. Fathi told me that when a ship was in port unloading, there would be a steady stream of large trucks on this road.

The mountains were beautiful with spectacular scenery. Many of the mountainsides were terraced to preserve the soil and moisture. Many farms were in evidence at the higher elevations where corn, vegetables, fruit, and tea were raised on the terraced slopes. The higher we climbed, the more moisture there was and the greener the fields and forest. Soon we were in the clouds with mist and rain obscuring the view. Animals were beside, and on, the road almost continually with an accompanying shepherd. Some flocks, especially goats, numbered in the hundreds. We passed several small towns and wayside restaurants with crowds of people walking about, some donkey carts, and the usual flock of animals being driven to market or to greener pastures.

Figure 112

Animals on the Road

Figure 113
Terraced Farms

Figure 114

Above the Clouds

Figure 115

Baboons on the Road

Asmara, Eritrea, to Michigan, USA

After several hours of grinding climbs, turns, and stops for animals, we arrived at the beautiful city of Asmara. There was a smoking dump at the entrance, stinking to high heaven. There was also a thorough checkpoint at the entry, asking for permits, passports, and a look at your belongings before you entered the city. The city, located at 6000 feet, was cool and refreshing, but not cold, with a bright sun shining on lots of well-dressed people. From 2:00 to 5:00 p.m. almost everyone rests. Evening brings everyone out in force with theater, restaurants, buses, and sidewalks packed with people. There were many young people just out for the night. A person would be happy and safe all night. Old ladies sat on corners selling nuts, candy, newspapers, paper products etc. until all hours of the morning, in complete safety and doing a good business.

Fathi took me to his beautiful home, which had every modern appliance, to sleep. But first, he took me out to his cousin's restaurant for a large, five-course, fish dinner.

The next day, Fathi took me to one of his friend's stores and explained what we needed. The friend came with us, giving directions from store to store, until we found the bearing I was looking for. I paid too much, as I accepted the first price offered, while my friend was bargaining for a lower price. He was a bit upset that I paid what I did. The part was almost the same as the original, but needed a bit of machining to bring it to the exact size. He knew exactly where to go and it was machined that afternoon to the exact specifications. The rest of the day, we went from business to business, while Fathi delivered and purchased supplies. Our last stop was to pick up Salaam (means peace) to work for Fathi as a waitress in the Massawa Hotel.

The trip back to Massawa was much more uncomfortable, as Fathi needed to stop often to rest, eat, and drink a whiskey or two. The fog was so thick I could not see the road, but Fathi kept going and, miraculously, we eventually arrived safely back in Massawa.

To gain a permit to travel to Thio took two full days. First, I was told, "No, go to Asmara and present the problem". I made a few calls to friends, who had friends, who made calls, and the next day was told my case was being reviewed. I had previously made friends with the head of security, who had been to the tulip festival in Holland, Michigan, and had attended the University of Michigan. Also I had made friends with a Catholic Priest who helped me. (I was surprised to learn that 50% of Eritreans are Christians.) By the time I arrived at security the next day, my trip had been approved and I was told to bring the papers and I would receive a security stamp.

The boys had left for India. Lo had spoken to Captain Jack of "Miss Cat", who was still in Massaw and told him he would leave my necessary papers for India in the Harbor of Salable in Oman. With the recommendation of Jack, I recruited Moussi, who agreed to be my crewmember to Massawa.

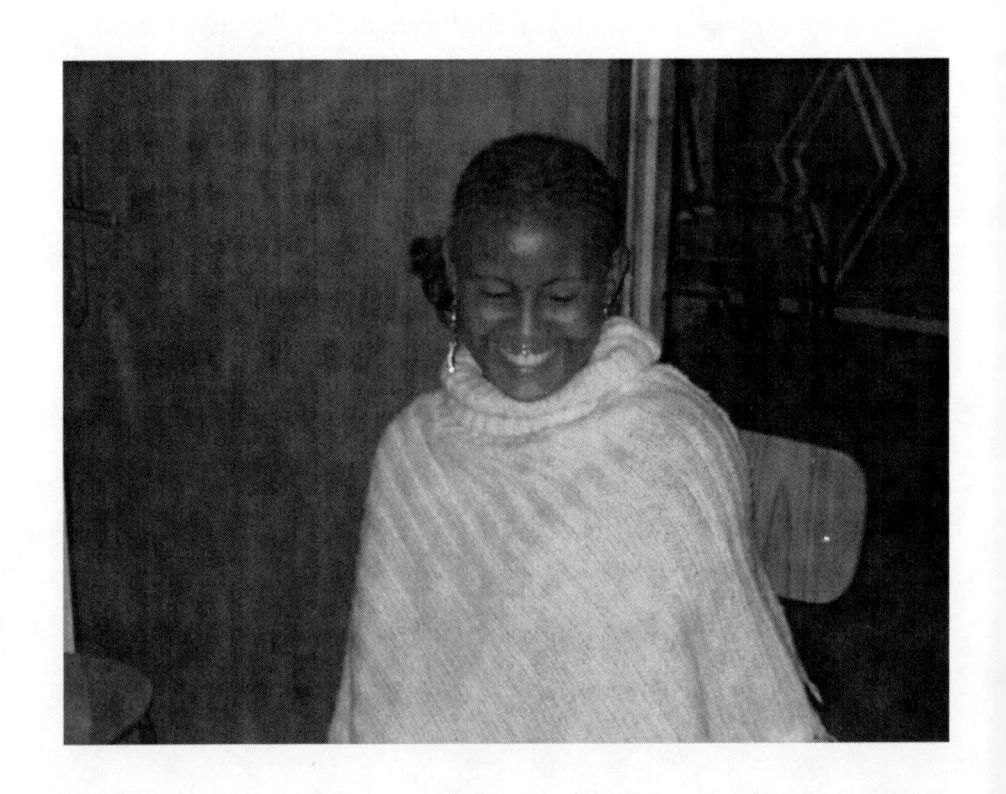

Figure 116

Salaam, New Waitress for the Massawa Hotel

Figure 117
Fathi, Owner of the Massawa Hotel

Moussi, a good-looking, six-foot Eritrean, had assisted Jack, a French charter sailboat Captain. Moussi had seaman's papers and a passport. I was staying at the Massawa Hotel, which was only a block from where he lived. We had previously met at the hotel and had become friends. He and Ben Zimmo had helped me with several small problems. He spoke English, Arabic, and his native tribe's language, Tigre.

He had been in the National Service of his country for three years and had fought in the thirteen-year Eritrea War of Independence against Ethiopia. He had fought in the horrendous battle of Nakfa City, for which the Eritrean currency is named. That battle was so intense that over 20,000 soldiers were killed on each side. Moussi had been wounded by mortar fire, with injuries to his head, body, and one leg, which was broken. He related to me stories of days without water or food and terrible suffering for long periods of time.

On the day we left Massawa, we awoke at 4:30 a.m. and caught a contract bus to the bus station. At 5:00 a.m., the Massawa to Thio Bus showed up and bedlam ensued as there were at least 60 people waiting for a 40-passenger bus. The seats had all been sold out the day before. All kinds of supplies were loaded on the roof of the bus; tables, chairs, bags of sugar, bags of salt, bags of grain, and a 30-foot ridgepole to build a new house. Goats were running around and looking for a handout.

We didn't have a ticket, so we were told to return tomorrow. However, a man told us to take the Toro bus and then walk out of town

Figure 118

Massawa to Assab Bus

away from the police and wait. Apparently the same story had been told to many, as we found a crowd of men and women walking up the mountain out of town. Sure enough, the same bus from Massawa came along, full of people, and stopped. There was a mad rush and Moussi propelled me up the steps and into the crowded bus. Sixteen of us plus live chickens, baggage, and a sack of produce all crowded onto the bus with standing room only.

We bounced along for a couple of hours and a man began to order the young people out of their seats and then gave the seats to the women and older men. So I had a seat with four other people, or a least one bun had a seat, with my knees high up in the air as my feet were on sacks of salt. It was much easier to get through checkpoints, as the isles were too crowded for the army to get through and they sometimes skipped us in the back of the bus. I also tried to sleep through checkpoints, covering up my white face, which at times worked well.

I had the same scenery as the first trip but now much less visible, sitting in the crowded bus looking around, over, or between people. The windows were not clean, except for the one that fell out completely, letting in blessed clean air with a touch of diesel fumes. The Eritreans hated a breeze and closed all the windows, regardless of the hot temperatures. They requested the driver to stop and a young fellow ran back and picked up the window, which was still in one piece. They taped cardboard over the window hole and off we went bouncing, swaying side-to-side, and roaring up and down the hills. The passengers only got interested when we saw wild deer or ostriches. It was uncomfortable, but I was on my way to "Idyllic"! The bus charged along bouncing, swaying, and at times, coming to a crawl speed to pass through a wash full of sand or rocks, all the time stopping to pick up more Arabs with their multiple wives, kids, and baggage. We arrived on the highway outside Thio at 9:00 p.m. and hunted up the local hotel, which consisted of a roof and 50 cots for 35 ERN ($2.30 USD) each.

The city of Thio is about five miles from the highway. We woke up early and waited for a taxi that didn't show up, so we began to walk. We walked the whole way, meeting about 300 school kids coming our way, each saying, "Good morning, how are you?"

After arriving at the Thio naval base, we arranged for a fisherman to take us back to "Idyllic" in Anfil Bay. Moussi and I, two fishermen, and the Naval Commander boarded an open fishing boat and off we went. Arriving at the fishermen's village, we picked up the fisherman/guard and then motored across the reef to "Idyllic", which was exactly as we had left her, nothing taken and nothing touched. They all stuck around to see if I could fix the engine, which I proceeded to do in the oppressive heat. My first try was unsuccessful, but with a small disassembly and readjustment, the engine ran perfectly.

The real catch came later when I tried to pay the guard. He asked for a completely exorbitant sum, 4,000 ERN ($277 USD). I didn't have that much money and told him so. We then discussed and negotiated the sum to slightly less than what I had, which was still

Figure 119
Thio Water System

Figure 120

Water Drums

Figure 121
Thio Main Street

Figure 122

Thio Market Scene

exorbitant, 800 ERN ($53 USD) plus 60 liters of fuel. I had no choice except to pay him.

Arriving at the boat, Moussi wanted to leave right away but I was dead tired, which I had a difficult time explaining to him. He suggested I drink some sugar water. I had traveled eight hours in a hot crowded bus, slept on a cot outdoors, walked five miles in the hot sun, repaired the engine while arguing with the fishermen, and was really tired. Finally I told him I was just too old to leave and this he accepted as a good excuse. I slept the entire night with the comfort of "Idyllic" gently rocking and the thought that everything was finally all right. We stayed anchored for the night and by morning I was revived.

On March 1st we left Anfil Bay and motored out to sea against heavy swells directly on the nose. We caught a good southerly wind once we were out of the harbor. I took a chance at one place and sailed behind an island to pick up a good wind. I cut closer to the reef than I should have and at once felt the stern scrape the coral and heard the depth alarm ringing. I could see coral just a few feet under us but we made it, by the skin of our teeth, to deeper water. Once clear of the reef and into deep water, we sailed with a brisk wind on our stern. We made wonderful time to Shumma Island where Moussi had predicted the wind would stop. The wind did stop there and the engine was necessary for the rest of the trip in to the pier. We arrived at Massawa at about 3:00 a.m. and tied up to the pier. I checked in with Customs and Immigration at 7:00 a.m. and was cleared to stay.

Moussi could not get permission to leave Eritrea, so I was left without a crew! Lo had warned us to sail only after midnight from

Massawa to Yemen in order to avoid the pirates who operated during daylight hours. I did not want to try the strait between Yemen and Somalia at night by myself. In addition, my finances were in bad shape, so I regretfully decided to put "Idyllic" on the hard at Massawa and go home to rest, to obtain crew, and to recoup my finances. I would have had to be in Aden, Yemen, by the 23rd of February in order to continue with the RSR and I had already missed that date. It was getting much too hot in that part of the world and soon would become unbearable for me. I had already lost 55 pounds during the trip. Eritrea, in the summer, is considered to be the hottest place on earth. I planned to return the next fall when it would be cooler. I had to set a date to leave for home before my visa expired on March 18th.

I had tied up to the port pier with tugs and freighters all around, loading and unloading. I had a visit from my friend, Atiq Ur Rehman, who was the chief cook on the M/V Hyderabad, a Pakistani ship that was carrying 15,800 tons of sugar from Brazil. It had been unloading for over two weeks, with each bag being handled by hand two times in the hot sun to load them onto truck trailers in the port. He invited me to dine with him on board the ship. He served me a delicious meal of rice and chicken, as I tried not to watch the parade of cockroaches marching around the walls and corners of the kitchen. He also invited me to look him up in Karachi, Pakistan.

On the next day, March 4th, I went to the Head Control Office of the Port. They had me fill in many papers declaring my tonnage, gross and net, and declare I had no passengers, no pets, no stowaways, and no drugs, and then list my stowaways with nationality and legal status, etc.

I spent that evening with Moussi and his friend Ben Zimmo. First for tea and then for argument, as they say, about Moussi's pay. We agreed on $100 USD per month. When that was settled, we went separate ways to avoid suspicion and met at a restaurant to watch a football game on TV. We bought tea and hot roasted peanuts there. Later in the evening, I returned to the "Idyllic", made some popcorn, and went to bed. I started to wash my laundry the next day, as Moussi's wife, being on holiday, had refused the job. I did two loads of the laundry in a five-gallon bucket.

I visited Moussi's house, which is very old and run down. It had been built by the Turks under the Ottoman Empire's occupation of Eritrea. Stairs, all wooden and broken, slanting at an odd angle, worn by use through the centuries, and unlit at night, led to their rooms on the third floor. Upon entering the third floor, I stepped into an open roofed room about 20 x 20 feet, which is shared by other families in the building, whose children were playing there.

His lively, five-year-old daughter and his 25-year-old wife, who is small and thin like most Eritreans, greeted me. She had a smile from ear to ear, beautiful eyes, and pure white teeth. She had everything ready for a traditional coffee ceremony with everything set out; coffee beans, cups, and saucers. The charcoal was already lit.

After about an hour, the coffee was ready. The consistency of light syrup, it was poured into small cups and served with two spoonfuls of sugar. The whole ceremony was completed with delicacy

Figure 123

Moussi and Wife at Home

Figure 124

Grinding Coffee Beans

Figure 125

Moussi's Wife and Daughter

Figure 126
Moussi

and pride in the tradition. You are obligated to drink three cups. Any less and the host would be upset. Popcorn was served on a woven straw mat along with the coffee. Alongside the charcoal on the table was a small incense burner giving off a prodigious quantity of smoke. The wood for the incense burner was rare and expensive, having been imported from Ethiopia.

Over tea the next day, I learned why the fishermen had asked so much money for guarding "Idyllic" at Anfil Bay. It seems a German captain had hired two Egyptian crewmembers to help sail south in the Red Sea. Around Anfil Bay, he was found dead and the crewmembers anchored the boat. An investigation was made and the results indicated there was no evidence of foul play. The boat stayed for several months anchored in the bay with the fishermen watching it. When the owners showed up, they were so appreciative of the fishermen that they gave them a tremendous amount of money, probably from the insurance settlement. Thus when I showed up, they had expected the same amount of money and were severely disappointed by my settlement.

I started to decommission "Idyllic" while I was at the pier where it was easy to work. I took off the spray hood, the mainsail, and the genoa, folding and bagging them. I stowed them away in the V-birth. I also deflated the dinghy and folded it up into a roll, lowering it through the forward hatch into the V-birth also. I changed the oil and oil filter, a big messy, dirty job and finished the laundry that I had started. I had everything done by 4:00 p.m.. Then I walked over to the Massawa hotel and ordered my favorite mango and ice cream drink.

The next day, I went to the Massawa Hotel and had a small dish of chocolate ice cream. I met Moussi there and we talked about sailing the next year. That night, I met with the marina owner at the Beaches Restaurant. He said he could not get a crane and I would have to get my own. I checked the water at his marina and found that the depth was only 1.24 meters, not enough to float "Idyllic". I decided to cancel the work at his marina and go to the Government Ship Repair Yard for the take out, as they had excellent experience and more facilities than I could ever need. A place had been prepared already at the marina for "Idyllic" with a cradle already in place. I felt both bad and good about the decision.

When I went to the port to discuss the prospect of using the port's crane to lift "Idyllic" out of the water at the shipyard, I met with the usual bureaucratic red tape. It would be necessary to write a letter of request to do so and receive the Engineering Office's approval, signature, and stamp. Then, I would need the Port Director's signature, requiring a trip across town and a personal interview with him. Finally, I would have to pay in advance at the Port Technical and Financial Office. Initially the government officials wanted $600 per month to store the boat. However, I was able to negotiate this down to only $300 USD per month.

I went to the Port Manager, and then to Customs to get written permission for a currency exchange, and then to the bank to cash the needed traveler's checks, and finally to the Financial Office at the shipyard and paid 5100 ERN ($340 USD) cash for the use of the crane. Credit cards are not valid in Eritrea. I was scheduled to take "Idyllic"

Figure 127

Massawa Dockfronts

to the shipyard at 11:00 a.m. where she would be taken out at 12:00 noon. Moussi and I motored "Idyllic" over to the shipyard and tied her up to their jetty. By 1:00 p.m., "Idyllic" was out of the water, safe and secure on land. They said I could not stay on board, but changed their mind when we asked again that night, so I slept on 'Idyllic" for the next few days.

I made final arrangements to leave on March 7th. I found coolant for the engine for 400 ERN ($27 USD). Moussi came to the boat to help me prepare the outboard and diesel engine for storage. As a final task, we also washed the boat with fresh water to remove the salt. I had a good nights sleep on board that night with only a few mosquitoes to bother me.

On March 8, 2008, I took a plane out of Asmara, Eritrea, to Kartoum, Sudan, to Aden, Yemen, to London to Detroit and then took a Budget rental car from Detroit Metro to Montague. I found Michigan still in the winter season with ice and snow covering everything. This was quite a contrast from the 100-degree weather in Eritrea. It was damp and cold, and I was wearing light summer clothes. It took me several months to get warm, and even as I was writing this I was covered with an electric blanket and had my stocking cap on.

During this trip I lost 55 pounds, which is a lot of weight. It's normal for me to lose about 20 pounds on a sailing trip. My calorie intake decreases due to eating less red meat, less fatty food, and no pork products. This, with a sharp increase in physical exercise, both at sea and on land, results in a healthier lifestyle. In a small sailboat at sea, it is difficult to cook large amounts of food. Snacking on sandwiches and fruit is easier. In strange ports, a lot of walking and exploring for supplies is required, in addition to sightseeing. These factors all result in a loss of excess weight.

There were some disadvantages to joining the Red Sea Rally. When in the rally, one is more or less restricted to the schedule set by the organizer. I was not used to this and almost never had set a schedule for "Idyllic". The few times that I did, I later regretted having done so. We were not required to keep to the rally schedule, but if we didn't, we missed out on some events and lost many of the economic benefits of the rally.

The English language was required for all radio and official correspondence within the rally; however, many other non-English languages were used, causing some confusion and hard feelings within the group. Some captains really could not speak English at all. This resulted in tensions, as well as feelings from past events such as wars in Europe. When in a large group there are always some interpersonal problems, which come up over a period of time.

With respect to the dangers of traveling, I had the feeling that large groups of foreigners attracted problems, from the overzealous sellers to the possible terrorists who occupy these lands. A large group of rich sailors attracts attention from greedy officials, local thieves, bums, and illegal black market individuals.

Several hundred euros were required to join the rally, and since I was not able to share in the entire rally, I lost a lot of the value I had paid for. Last but not least, I lost a part of the independence that I had been used to in previous years.

The following is the "Vasco Da Gama Rally Musique" created by the French on the sailboat "Mylias", which we sang in English, French, and Dutch at our gatherings:

It's a famous rally
That is underway
Hisse oh! Vasco Da Gama
Twenty boats, thirty-nine sailors
I am proud to be here
One of them

Hold tight the tiller
And hold tight the wind
Hisse oh! Vasco Da Gama
If God wants, always straight ahead
We will go as far as
Mo-om-bai

Leaving for many months
Way from my country
Hisse oh! Vasco Da Gama
Thinking with sadness in our hearts
As we pass the light
Of Port Said

> One day we'll come back
> The head full of dreams
> Hisse oh! Vasco Da Gama
> Loaded with fabulous presents
> For all of my family and friends

In the Red Sea area, the food is poor, unsanitary, and often hard to obtain. Food covered with flies is not appetizing. The water is always suspect and sometimes turns green in a container. All of the RSR sailors had dysentery problems. These things discouraged overeating. Joe and Nico ate vegetarian diets with fish and chicken, but no meat. They enjoyed cooking these low-calorie meals. We only ate two meals a day while sailing. The heat of over 100 degrees decreased our appetites. Activity ceased in the area during the mid-day hours.

Infection from coral cuts and ocean water became prevalent and was hard to cure. I took a broad-spectrum antibiotic that helped considerably. The stress of having an inexperienced crew kept me on edge and I was unable to get proper rest when sailing. The slightest sail or course change required my attention. I had to worry about them keeping a sharp lookout at the helm and staying on course. In addition, the navigation was stressful because of all of the uncharted reefs. The boys did learn fast and I was able to relax more as the trip progressed.

So ended my adventures of the winter of 2007-8, sailing to Israel, Egypt, Sudan, and Eritrea. This was not the most enjoyable adventure I have had, but one that will live in my memory for a long time to come. It was, by far, the most difficult and frustrating sail of my career to date.

I logged 1923 miles on this leg for a total of about 25,783 miles on my trip around the world the wrong way.

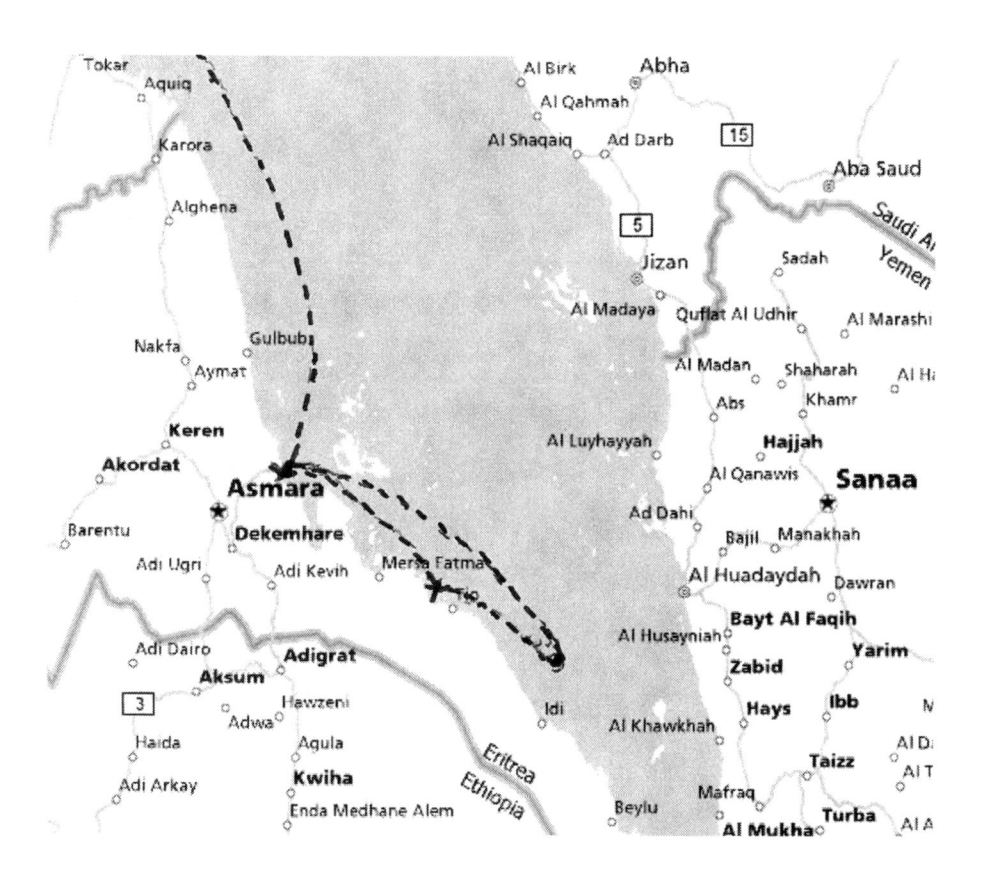

Figure 128

Route from Oseif, Sudan, to Massawa, Eritrea

CHAPTER XII - RETURN TO ERITREA

Trip to Eritrea

I left my home in Michigan Saturday, October 21, 2008, to return to my boat, "Idyllic", in Massawa, Eritrea, and continue my journey around the world. The last words my wife said were that, "If I got into difficulties I should give the boat away to free us of liability for its expense." This was a shock to me and that advice was both repulsive and unexpected.

I got off on the wrong foot when I rented a Budget rental car in Muskegon, 20 minutes from my home. While I waited at the agency for the attendant to show up, I had breakfast with my wife at Russ's restaurant. Finally, after an hour, a sleepy girl showed up at the agency and rented me a Nissan Altima, which could only be paid for by credit card. About half way to Chicago I looked down and realized I was driving a small Toyota. What a shock! How would I be treated on the other end? Upon arriving, the attendant did not even blink when I told her that I had the wrong car; "no problem sir", just like it happens every day.

My flight was in the evening, so I arrived much too early and had to impatiently wait out the day. I flew from Chicago to London without any problem but then had to wait the entire day for my next leg to Sana'a, Yemen. Then I had to stay in Yemen until the following day for my last leg to Asmara, Eritrea. Sana'a, shown in Figure 129, is Yemen's largest city with a population of over 1.8 million. Yemen Airlines put me up free in the Almusafir Hotel for the night. Figure 130 shows the entrance to the hotel; Figure 131 shows the front desk there; Figure 132 shows the Internet terminals; and Figure 133 shows the restaurant washroom.

I was warned that I needed a Yemeni visa before I could leave and I argued that the Yemeni visa was unnecessary as I was only passing through Yemen. They seemed to agree but as soon as I arrived at the hotel, I was handed a message to return and buy my visa so I took a taxi to the airport and purchased a Yemeni visa for $60. I also was shocked when they told me I could not leave until I possessed an Eritrean visa also. Hiring the taxi to the Eritrean Embassy was an exercise in frustration because the driver did not speak English and could not find the Embassy. We ended up at the Ethiopian Embassy where another taxi took me to the right destination. Figure 134 shows a private taxi. By the time I arrived, three hours later, they were closed for the weekend and would not open until Monday. As my flight had been scheduled for that Friday, I had to go to the Yemeni Airlines office to change my reservation to the following Tuesday. I was afraid there would be a large penalty charge but was surprised to find the change was free.

On Monday morning, the embassy told me a visa was not available and I was unable to continue to Eritrea. I called my friend,

Figure 129

Sana'a, Yemen

Figure 130

Entrance to Hotel Almusafir

Figure 131

Hotel Almusafir Front Desk

Figure 132

Internet at Hotel

Figure 133

Hotel Washroom

Figure 134

Private Taxi

Sahle, the shipyard financial manager in Eritrea, and finally made contact with him on Monday. He agreed to write a letter to Foreign Service to help me obtain a visa. I then had to wait to hear from the Embassy.

For something to do while waiting, I began to study my new Garmin GPS using the handbook as a guide. Later, I went out for a pizza at a nearby restaurant. I noted many jambiya, the name given to the curved dagger that Yemeni men wear so proudly in their wide belts. Positioned directly in the middle of the stomach for maximum impact, it is never covered by clothes. A well-wrought jambiya, with a saifani hilt made from the horn of the rhinoceros, can cost up to $1,000,000 USD. A rhinoceros horn, illegal as a protected species, can fetch up to $1500 USD per kilogram in Sana'a. An ordinary Jambiya may cost only $1 USD. Men, above the age of 14, typically wear the Jambiya as an accessory to their clothing. The quality of the hilt denotes their social status. Figure 135 shows a man with a rhinoceros horn Jambiya. Figure 136 shows a man with his wife and child on a sidewalk in Sana'a. Figure 137 shows me in a souvenir store. Figures 138 and 139 show street vendors in Sana'a. Figure 140 shows a Sana'a street scene. Figure 141 shows goats being driven to market on the streets of Sana'a.

The call to prayer, La ill aha il Allah, Muhammad u rasal ullah, (There is no God but Allah and Muhammad is his messenger) issued from the loudspeakers five times each day. I used the word "Inshallah" (meaning If God wills) very often.

Figure 135

Man with Rhinoceros Horn Jambiya

Figure 136

Man with Wife and Child

Figure 137

Harold in Souvenir Store

Figure 138
Street Vender

Figure 139

Street Salesman

Figure 140

Sana'a Street Scene

Figure 141

Goats on the Street

While I was trapped in Sana'a, Yemen, without a visa for Eritrea, a cyclone came bringing thirty hours of heavy thunderstorms and torrential rains. The news reports said 61 people had been killed and more were expected when the rescuers reached the isolated villages. Mud-brick buildings were no match for the floodwaters and soon melted and collapsed under the pressure of rains and flooding river. The streets in the city were like rivers. The number of homes lost had reached 26,000 and more were to be counted. Rescue efforts were being made by helicopters and the army, but many people had not been reached at that time. I survived, seven stories up in the Yemeni Airways Hotel (Almusafir Hotel), and didn't even get my feet wet.

While I was waiting, I checked my money belt and found my traveler's checks missing! Where they had gone was a mystery as I had kept them with me at all times, with great caution, wherever I went. Except for the dollars in my pocket, this was all the money that I had to make my journey. I tried to contact American Express. The contact number was in London, in another time zone, and I never heard from them. I had enough cash with me to last a short time, but since credit cards were not accepted in Eritrea, I did not have enough money to continue my trip without the traveler's checks. I called my wife, Vonda, who called American Express. They insisted on talking to me. Vonda supplied them with a phone number and name at the shipyard where I could be contacted, but they did not seem eager to contact me and I did not hear from them. E-mail was not permitted in Eritrea. The U.S. State Department had increased its warning to avoid travel to

Eritrea and advised that the U.S. Embassy would no longer assist anybody outside the city of Asmara. I was becoming desperate to obtain funding for my trip.

On October 28 a week of worry had gone by and I still had not seen "Idyllic." I thought maybe news would come on that day. I called the Embassy and to see if there was any development. There was still no visa as both telephone and fax communications had been cut off by the storm. The front desk personnel had warned me that this delay would happen. They have seen it before when an American flew to Asmara and had to leave until he could get a visa.

Saleh Abobakr Bazara, the hotel manager, reduced my room charge from $25 to $15 per day to help me out. After I took a picture of the hotel restaurant manager, shown in Figure 142, he also took an interest in my case and tried to help. He offered me special-cooked, American food -- far better than the Yemeni food -- American omelets, fried with tomatoes and onions, and hamburgers made out of goat meat between long loaves of bread. There were many strange dishes with unidentified contents. Where normally everyone was given one loaf of bread and one boiled egg, I received two of each.

I heard on October 29 that the floods had so far killed over 100 people. I went across town by taxi to the fortress called the American Embassy and found guards and armored vehicles surrounding it, because they had been attacked only a few weeks before. There were bullet holes in some of the walls and buildings. I was met by a guard at the gate and escorted to a tent where security agents took my passport and identification into the complex. Next I was escorted to a

Figure 142

Hotel Restaurant Manager

reception room where a diplomat interviewed me. His staff checked into my case and reported that it was only a matter of time and they could not speed up the procedure or really help in any way. I walked to the airlines office to change my ticket, once again at no charge.

On October 30 my hopes were waning. If I couldn't get to the "Idyllic", I was spinning my wheels, spending money uselessly, and getting nowhere. I racked my brain trying to find solutions to my problem and only came up with the answer of waiting longer and being patient with the system! I went out for a roasted chicken dinner for $4. Then I had to change my ticket once again.

A week later, I still did not have any news of my visa to Eritrea. I had been told that all that was required was a telephone call from the shipyard manager to the Eritrean Foreign Service who would call the Eritrean Embassy in Yemen. I was really beginning to doubt they ever intended to let me in at all. Finally, after 15 days of waiting, a call came from the Embassy that I could come in and pick up my passport and visa for Eritrea! I quickly called a taxi and off I went. I received a business visa for three months as a reward for waiting so long.

On my last day in Yemen, November 4, I was able to play tourist for the first time, after fifteen days of hard work, frustration, and worry. The power continued to go off and on for short periods of time but that day it was off for a long time and did not return before I left. I returned to the airport via hotel bus, this time equipped with visa; however, no one checked to see if I had one or not, at least not in Yemen, but I was sure they would in Eritrea.

Figure 143

African Pension

I arrived at the Asmara, Eritrea, airport at 1:00 a.m. and filled in an immigration card and sheet declaring the amount of money that I was bringing into the country. I took a taxi for 300 ERN to the African Pension, shown in Figure 143, where I had spent the night on my previous trip. It cost me 180 ERN per night for a Stage 2 room.

The African Pension (hotel) was located in a district a few blocks from downtown making walking to all destinations rather easy. The location was directly across from the Italian Embassy, so it was pretty well guarded by armed guards 24 hours a day. I arrived late and found the guard sleeping in the guardhouse on the street level. After being aroused, he helped me with my bags, as the hotel was 50 feet up some steps. The front desk attendant was sleeping on the floor behind the counter and when awakened, he said, "Please come back in the morning!"

The hotel itself is an old Italian-style mansion, formerly the Mayor's residence, surrounded by formal gardens, fairly well kept up with statues, flowers and greenery. The hotel had many rooms. Stage 1, the best rooms, costing 230 ERN, were large rooms with a ceiling fan and double beds. Stage 2 rooms, for 180 ERN, were just a shade smaller. Stage 3 rooms were the same but upstairs. Stage 4 rooms were out back in a shed occupied by the workers and when I requested one, I was told it was occupied; however, when I insisted, one finally became available for 130 ERN. The WC, for both sexes, was large with two toilets, two private showers, one lavatory, and no soap or toilet paper. Each toilet had a bucket of water and a small scoop for washing and flushing. Toilet paper was available from the front desk for 13 ERN.

The TV was in the reception room and only the ERTV channel is available unless someone went onto the roof and changed the direction of the antenna dish. Everything was clean, old, and worked most of the time. The electricity went on and off, as in the rest of the city. The staff was very friendly and spoke fairly good English.

The Eritrea Customs kept the spare boat parts I had brought and told me to come back the next day, which I did and then they said, "Maybe tomorrow." Each time customs said they would call my taxi driver and he would call me to go to airport and pick things up. So I returned again, each time paying a 300 ERN taxi fare. I went from office to office, always with its paper shuffle, stamps, signatures, and finally a 234 ERN charge for customs and then 300 ERN for the agent. I did learn however that the public bus would cost only 1 ERN, but a kind man returned me to the hotel free.

On November 6th, I awoke early and walked to town for tea and a donut for 8 ERN. The bank offered 15 ERN per dollar but the black market payed 28 ERN with plenty of sidewalk salesmen; however one had to be very careful not to get caught exchanging money. At nine o'clock I went to the Foreign Visitors Office and applied for a travel permit to Massawa. They told me to return the next day and it would be ready. I looked around town and ate at a beef restaurant with the native workmen. I got a rather large bowl full of chopped beef and bread for 40 ERN. The most interesting aspect of the restaurant was the back wall covered by the hanging carcasses of several cows, from

Figure 144

Future Dinner at the African Pension

which the cook carves your meal. Of course a few flies dot the scene, beef, tables, walls, and ceiling.

I finally received a call to pick up the suitcase full of spare parts. When I arrived, I could not find a suitcase in a large room stacked from floor to ceiling with all manner of freight. I hunted for an hour restacking cases until I found mine on the very bottom. Then I went from the storage room to the inspection room where an examiner went over every item asking its value, purpose, and a zillion questions; then, to an agent for the final tally of value and tax figures that took another hour of waiting; next, to the finance office for calculating, explanation, discussion, and payment of 250 ERN; then back to the examiner and agent for a payment of 300 ERN; and finally, back to storage where I received my bag after three hours of work. Afterward, I returned to the hotel with the patient taxi driver, who had spent the entire morning waiting for me.

The next day I arose early, packed, called a taxi, and left for the bus station at 7:00 a.m. I arrived none too early as the bus was packed with riders, many milling around outside with large piles of freight scattered about. I paid for a ticket and hoisted my heavy suitcase up on top of the bus. After much discussion and flailing of hands and arms, I was ushered to the front of the bus to sit next to the driver, a place reserved for important riders. Then climbing over freight, ladies, and miscellaneous obstacles, I finally landed in my plush seat, which had a large windscreen, to see the sights on the road to Massawa.

Difficulties in Continuing

In Massawa, the shipyard siren goes off every day at 6 a.m. waking the dead and giving a clue that daylight is coming. The object is to get an early start before the sun is up bright and hot, making work hard to near impossible. The temperature rises by noon to 100 degrees or more in the shade and hotter in the sun. "Idyllic" offered a shade from the sun where many shipyard workers could be found resting and hiding from the supervisors. I took the dingy, fenders, and sails out of the V-berth Friday morning and started the pumping up and assembly of the dingy. I attempted to install a brand-new water pump, but I needed better connectors, which were not available. I then installed the spray hood, which took about an hour. Afterwards I went for a late breakfast. The next day I received electrical service at the boat, but then it went off as usual. I completed the installation of the water pump and it worked fine.

On November 12, I received a bill with a charge of $20 for electric hookup and $20 for the stepladder. This is more than anywhere else I have been in the world and completely unreasonable. However they did have a good repair shop capable of any work that I needed and an excellent, well-trained labor force.

It was very hot, 100 degrees or more in the shade, making it impossible for me to function. Being from Michigan, I was not acclimated to that heat. The Africans tolerate the heat very well.

When I was here last year, Moussi had agreed to go with me to Yemen. Moussi's wife said he had all the papers necessary for going.

Sahle, who also wanted to go, had no money, no good passport and no permission to leave.

I went to town and had traditional coffee with Moussi's wife. She said he was in Asmara and would return that night. The traditional coffee ceremony is practiced regularly in most homes and can be ordered in restaurants. Usually a lady starts a small charcoal fire in a container about a foot high and a foot wide. When it's burning well, raw coffee beans are placed in a small metal pan with a long handle over the coals and roasted to perfection. While smoking, the pan is passed under each person's nose to smell the aroma and it's proper to make a positive comment about the good smell. When roasted, the beans are inspected and the poor ones are discarded. Then the beans are poured into a wooden container and pounded with a metal rod until they reach the consistency of powder. This is poured into a small clay pot with a long neck. Water is added and the pot is placed on the glowing charcoal to boil. When steam is coming out of the neck, the contents are inspected and sometimes more water is added. Small teacups, such as used in dollhouses, are washed and placed, with their small plates, near the server. A plug made of horsehair is placed in the neck of the clay pot to strain out the grounds and the coffee, close to the consistency of syrup, is poured into the cups. Two spoonfuls of sugar are added to each cup and the first cup is handed to the guest. It's expected that a comment will be made about the delicious coffee. If not, the contents are thrown away and a new batch is made, usually consuming another hour. It's polite to drink a minimum of three cups or else the host is offended. Sometimes when I was sick it took a long time to consume my quota, of which some was always spilled, hopefully without notice. This ceremony was practiced all over Eritrea and one had to be careful, if in a hurry, to decline an invitation. On a few occasions, when walking the back streets, I was invited to have coffee with some lady who was trying to attract a husband. Figure 145 shows the coffee being prepared and Figure 146 show me drinking the coffee.

On November 16th, I arose to the ship repair yard's siren at 6:00 a.m. as usual and went to work immediately. The project for the day was to hook up the exhaust system, but I soon found I needed hoses of a larger size than the old ones, which were useless. Much later, after asking numerous people, I was able to finish the job quickly when I finally obtained hoses, rescued from the junk pile by my old mechanic in the port shop, for a price.

The Captain of the fuel ship, Beulia, invited me for dinner one day and I accepted with relish. Moussi, who now worked on that fuel ship for the Eritrea Shipping Lines, prepared the fresh-caught fish, which were delicious. I ate with the captain in the officer's salon. Following the meal, I watched the "Robinson Crusoe" movie with the crew.

November 17th started with a queasy feeling in my stomach and by 10:00 things had really begun to churn. I had been very careful to eat only well-cooked food and to drink only pure, bottled water, but apparently these precautions were not sufficient. Everything began exiting my body in whatever direction it could find. I'm not sure but what my ears were even running wild. "Idyllic" was not in the water

Figure 145

Coffee Ceremony

Figure 146

Drinking Coffee

so a pail of seawater was all I had to catch the vomit, which was the consistency of seawater but brown. This lasted three days and caught the attention of the yard staff who insisted on putting me in the hospital. I assured them I would be all right and had medicine for such a malady. Sahle Noor and Saleh of the financial department were so concerned they went out and bought an oral rehydration salt (ORS) from UNICEF. Sahle also insisted that I come to his home where I could be better watched and taken care of. I was too weak to resist. His home was substantial with a comfortable bed in the dining area under a wonderful ceiling fan, which kept me cool and free of flies and mosquitoes. They tried to force feed me but this only complicated my condition. The management of the shipyard, especially the head of the technical department, was worried that I was dying. I guess my appearance was not the best. I began taking Flagyl from my medical supplies and this soon started to keep water and a bit of food down. My strength gradually returned during the three wonderful days at Sahle's home. On the third day, Sahle was informed by management and security sources that they wanted me on the boat where they could better monitor my comings and goings. So I returned to "Idyllic".

I was able to go back to work as usual on November 20. Finding hoses for the exhaust system became a citywide search. After waiting for the shipyard for a week, I took things into my own hands and traveled across the island to the Port of Massawa where Ibreham, a good mechanic, had helped me before. I gave him a sample of what I needed and he promised to help and asked that I meet him aboard an Egyptian ship in the harbor, as the port did not look too kindly on supplying private parties with port materials. The next day he came with a bag full of the right sized hoses, which I paid him 300 ERN for. I then began the assembly of the exhaust system with all new parts from America and hoses from Ibreham. With the help of a shipyard mechanic, the two-week struggle was successfully finished in an hour, much to my relief. With the trip to the port and an hour's work upside down in the bilge, I was exhausted and spent the rest of the day swatting flies and trying to rest in the shade under "Idyllic" on a mat. Between sleeps, I swam in the 75-degree water for short periods of time.

The next day I tackled the installation of the heat exchanger. This project was "old hat" as I had done this on several occasions last season. The task took only an hour using the new exchanger I had purchased at home and hand carried to "Idyllic." To celebrate I took a minivan taxi ride to town and the market, shown in Figure 147, where I bought goodies such as oranges, small bananas, potatoes and onions. It was difficult to convince the ladies that I needed only a few and I ended up with a kilo of each. Figures 148-150 show different parts of the market. Chickens and eggs are available from the street markets shown in figures 151 and 152. On the return trip I purchased roasted peanuts from a small stand near the bus stop, one ERN for a handful.

Returning to the yard I visited with my friends in the financial department who had fresh water and an air conditioner. I stayed until closing time at the 1:30 p.m. siren. I rested again under "Idyllic" with my usual swim and shower for the rest of the afternoon. In the

Figure 147

Massawa Market

Figure 148

Grain Market

Figure 149

Spice Market

Figure 150
Fruit Market

Figure 151

Chickens For Sale

Figure 152

Eggs For Sale

evening I went to the local café and joined the enthusiastic crew watching England's premier football league game.

You either like eating Eritrea food or you don't. Injera, a traditional food there, shown in Figure 153, is a large circular pancake, gray in color that is used as a carrier for all other foods. A large variety of sauces and stews, generally known as wat, are scooped up on the middle of the top half. One then breaks off a chunk of the injera, dips the sauce from the middle, and pops it into his mouth. It can be mild to hot, made with vegetables, goat, camel, chicken, eggs, and liver or tripe. On some occasions, a young lady or the hostess fed me by hand, depending on the situation, to impress me or to make sure I was really satisfied.

Eating with your fingers was almost always practiced and cleanliness was assured by being provided with a bowl and a pitcher of water, which was poured over your hands. This was repeated at the end of the meal to clean the food off your hands. No napkins were provided.

Beer is made by the women, who mix grains and bake them into a flat, circular loaf, which is then crushed and fermented to make the beer. Figure 153 shows the beer mix loaf baking on a small stove.

About that time it became clear to me that a crewmember was not readily available and not likely to become available. This was not a surprise as the same problem occurred last year. Moussi was my best bet as he had a seaman's card, passport, and permission to sail; however, because of my delay in arriving he had found a berth on the

Figure 153

Baking Beer Mix

fuel tanker of the Eritrean Shipping Lines. Sahle, although he said he wanted to go, had done nothing to prepare during all those months and only after I had arrived, had applied for renewal of his passport. He said he did not have any money for it before. Nasser in Yemen wanted to go but many complications would have arisen in his getting to Massawa. So I was back to square one -- a boat ready to depart but with no crew available.

An interesting metrological phenomenon known as the intertropical convergence zone occurs almost exactly at the port of Massawa. The northern section of the Red Sea has predominately north winds, which I rode down almost all the way last year, with the exception of a few calm days with no wind. Arriving in the area of Massawa, the winds died leaving an area of calm or slight south winds. That area is the zone where the north winds meet the south winds or converge with them. Sometimes one will experience north winds, but more often south winds. The month I was there, south winds blew exclusively except for a few morning hours. Trying to go south, one needs to motor or wait long periods of time for a favorable wind, or no wind, to make southward movement. The cruising guide and wind direction guides give the percentages of this phenomenon.

I was well aware that the Somali pirates were the biggest obstacle to sailing in the Gulf of Aden. Four freighters had just been attacked and captured, 32 were anchored in Somalia waiting for ransom for the crews and ships. One Saudi Arabian tanker, with a million dollars of fuel on board, had been taken and the attackers were asking 25 million dollars in ransom. That week an American cruise ship, with over a thousand passengers, was attacked. Thank heaven they outran the attackers' small boats. My dear wife said that if "Idyllic" were to be taken, she would pay no ransom and inform the poor pirates that Harold would be their responsibility and to keep him. A very unpleasant thought, although joining the pirates would probably be my one chance in life to become rich!

That pirate situation, combined with my location in a third world country, made finding a crewmember nearly impossible. The horrible thought kept popping up that my wife's parting words were, "Just give away the boat to a friend, end your liability, and return home." This I refused to do but the thought kept preying on my mind. What if I offered the boat up for sale? Talking this over with friends, I was advised against it as no one in Eritrea had any hard currency other than ERN. This put me between a rock and a hard place.

Sunday I met a Swiss captain, Stefan Zueger, who began to pour out his troubles with the girls of Massawa and his unfortunate luck in the recent cyclone. Although the storm was not nearly as severe in Massawa as it was in Yemen, it was still strong. The authorities had refused to let him go to a safe anchorage, requiring him to moor against the exposed freighter pier. During the storm, his small sailboat kept crashing against the concrete pier, even washing up onto the top of the pier. Slamming against the pier caused his fenders to burst, allowing the fiberglass hull to smash directly against concrete. The end result, which he showed me, was a two-inch, open crack, running fifteen feet along the rub rail where the deck and hull meet. Repair material was not available in Massawa and there wasn't anyone there with the skill required to repair such extensive damage. He attempted to go to the ship repair yard, but getting a boat craned out on the hard is a complicated task and the depth of the water there is less than his boat required. He had just given up. He had offered his boat, which he purchased for 20,000 EU, to a German captain for 1 EU. This offer was accepted and Stefan was planning to return home, broke and saddened by the turn of events.

This depressing news and other worse events started me thinking about selling "Idyllic." I was not willing to give up my dream and my boat like this. I thought there must be a better way. Stefan would have sailed with me, but he wanted to leave immediately and all I could promise was at least a week before I would be ready. I was a little too late with too little to offer. I really would have liked to have some of his equipment, such as the power anchor winch, radar, gas stove, etc.

The next evening Stefan and I went to a great fish restaurant, Salaam (peace), for grilled fish made in a wood-fueled oven. The cost was 110 ERN -- a bit expensive but well worth the cost. I went again several times and each time the price was lower, the last time down to 60 ERN (about $4 USD).

That night Stefan informed me that the next morning he was leaving for home and this was a goodbye dinner. The boat was still moored against the pier and he was unsure what would happen to it. Many fishing boats lie rotting along the shore stripped of equipment, motor, etc. I wondered if this would happen to that beautiful little sailboat.

Although I didn't have a great confidence in selling my boat, I thought it might be an option worthy of a try. I had asked the true value in other years, which had shocked potential buyers into backing away post haste. This time I thought I would offer her at a bargain price and see what happened. I informed everyone I met of this possibility; especially the shipyard management, freighter captains, and anyone interested who would listen. I was surprised in the interest and even received offers at my asking price, one from the College of Maritime Engineering for my exact asking price without any questions just, "yes we want it." I was warned by friends that only ERN was available that would have no value to me unless I stayed in the country, which I had no intention of doing. I needed USD that were almost impossible to find outside the Eritrean Government Treasury. However, two buyers persisted and even hinted that American money was not entirely impossible to come up with. They were both Italians who had outside connections for financing.

I had made friends with one of them before, as he had offered me a place to store "Idyllic" for the summer. He was in the hotel business and needed boats for the tourist trade. He had an ongoing, ten-year construction project of a new 5-star hotel. This buyer, his captain, and his chief mechanic visited the boat and asked a zillion questions. They asked for a list of additional equipment on board to study and promised to see me the next day with an idea for consideration. This sounded promising. However, the next day no one showed up. When Sahle called him to find out what happened, he was told that he was too busy to bother but maybe he would come the next day. Not an encouraging event but at least he didn't say, "No, not interested." The next day passed with the same results so I decided to take this into my own hands and pay a visit to the prospective buyer.

The next day, November 25, I obtained information on the location of the buyer and set out across town in mini-taxis to find his new hotel construction site. I had opposition from the guard, but eventually was allowed in to see the buyer. He was in a meeting with the Minister of Eritrean Economy. Interrupting the meeting, I approached the buyer and he made an offer far too low, but I accepted and we shook hands on it. He said he would come to the boat the next day. The next day, he didn't come but sent a message that he would show up at 9:00 a.m. the following day. Meanwhile the shipyard drew up a legal document with terms and conditions making the buyer liable for all of the storage cost and other expenses incurred by the sale, which amounted to several thousand dollars.

On November 26, the buyer showed up and discussed the terms of the agreement. He balked at the high expenses of storage and taxes. He received no sympathy from me, as his offer was exceedingly low. He said that he had very little American money but some Euros, which to me was even better as they were more valuable. We stepped aside to discuss the money and came to a full agreement, shook hands, and agreed to sign the legal documents in court the next morning.

The next morning he picked me up along with Sahle, the technical staff officer, Saleh, and a lawyer. We went to the courthouse where we signed numerous documents, all in Tirgue, of which I could not read a word. Everyone signed these documents and the court signed and stamped everything. The buyer and I then went to his office where he counted out the cash secretly, away from his staff, and gave it to me. Now I became responsible for thousands of US dollars and Euros stacked in neat bundles, which I stuffed in my computer case to take to the boat.

End of Cruise and Trip Home

The decision had been made, the die had been cast, and my dream of sailing around the world was ending, not in disaster as some do, but in a more planned, programmed way, not to my liking but final and sad. I was happy to be relieved of the responsibility for the boat, my life, and the lives of others who had sailed with me through the years. "Idyllic" and I had sailed for the last time; we had anchored permanently and changed to a different life. One is never really sure of the future, which turn one will take, what's around the corner, or how things will turn out. My around-the-world adventure is finished, never to resume. Halfway isn't bad, but far short of my goal.

This was probably for the best as my health and financial conditions were deteriorating at a faster pace than I could overcome by myself and help was not forthcoming. My wife and friends were relieved, with not one expressing disappointment and many saying I went too far and stopped almost too late.

Choosing what to save and what to leave was a chore I didn't enjoy. I had two bags to fill and the pile of to-go supplies was far too large for my small suitcases. Much of the food I gave to Moussi and Sahle. I gave some equipment to other friends who had helped and sold a few things for just pennies on the dollar. Much was inventory and left for the new owner to help operate "Idyllic". I had only a few hours to make big decisions and then I had to leave, as my visa was due to expire on December 4th. I had planned to leave on the morning of November 28th, but the owner asked me to stay and help with launching and moving the boat to its new berth.

The buyer, his captain, and his lawyer showed up early the next morning and announced that the crane from the port was coming at noon to launch "Idyllic" during the high tide. Everything went like clockwork. Several shipyard workers helped with the preparation and I virtually stood back and only gave directions and suggestions. Soon "Idyllic" was in the water floating prettily alongside a Navy patrol boat. We lined her out of the harbor over freighter lines that were lowered to let us pass. More than 35 workers, navy sailors, and the buyer's workers were yelling directions in their language making for a lively, well-organized effort. Soon we were tied to a mooring buoy outside the shipyard harbor. Trying to start the engine, we found the batteries too weak to turn it over. After bringing larger, more-powerful batteries, we found the engine to be frozen solid. A mechanic was called and he removed the head pan and injectors. He found fresh water in the injector holes, probably from the poor fuel that had water in it, which had been the case when refueling the year before. By this time it was getting dark, so we finished work and locked up for the evening.

After closing up the boat, I was given a ride to the central bus station where the buyer purchased a ticket for me to Asmara. I arrived in Asmara late at night and the boys had a fight on the roof of the bus over who was going to unload my suitcases. I gave the three boys 10 ERN each for their efforts. I then took a private car taxi to the African Pension for a well-deserved shower and night's rest.

The next morning I arose early, walked downtown to a small tea café, and had chai (tea) and a donut for 8 ERN. From there I walked to the Yemeni Airlines office and purchased a ticket for that evening's flight home for $840 USD. Egypt airlines wanted $1900 for the same trip while Lufthansa wanted $3000, so my choice was easily made.

I arrived at the airport early that evening as I envisioned as much trouble as I had last year and I wasn't disappointed. Security went through my baggage with a fine tooth comb; I think they were tipped off by the police from the court that I might have American dollars. They found these of course, which were far more than I was allowed to take out of the country. Two security agents interviewed me and one remained to suggest that maybe, for a small amount, he could be of some help passing me through. Two hundred USD did the trick and away I went. This was actually the first time I had paid baksheesh in Eritrea, but I had found it very common in Egypt.

I wrote the following letter to my good and helpful friend:
"Dear Sahle,

"It is with great regret that I was unable to spend the evening with you and your beautiful wife for a going away dinner. Please apologize to her for standing you up.

"We launched "Idyllic" and ran into engine problems; we worked until dark without success. Then Premo immediately took me to the bus station for a bus to Asmara. I tried repeatedly to call you without success to inform you of my situation. Arriving in Asmara late, I fell asleep at the

African Pension upon my arrival. The next morning I went to the Yemeni Airline office where they sold me a ticket and whisked me off to the airport immediately for my flight home without a chance to call, shave, or really gather my wits.

"Enclosed is a small amount which I owe you to pay for my phone calls.

With best regards and a big thank you!
Harold Knoll"

Homecoming on December 2, 2008, was sweet, as I had missed my wife and dogs at home. I was greeted by a winter storm such as I had experienced many times in Michigan with heavy wet snow, wind, and icy roads -- downright miserable winter conditions! While going through some clothes I had left at home, I discovered my American Express Traveler's checks! I don't know how I managed to leave home without them.

My life's odyssey had ended for lack of a water pump. If I had carried a spare water pump last year, I could have safely sailed, with my French crewmembers, up the notorious Gulf of Aden and across to Bombay with the Rally Group. Then this year I would have been beyond the terrorist activities in Bombay and on my way toward Australia. But my poker playing co-author tells me that's playing "Ifins", which is not allowed in poker or real life!

Thus ends my "Sailing Around the World the Wrong Way".